LIFE WITH ZIGGY:
A BOY, A DOG, & A LIFE SAVED

JUSTIN BARROW

Ziggy and Justin, September 2005

ISBN-13: 978-1493501205
ISBN-10: 1493501208

Dear Reader...

Owning our story can be hard but not nearly as difficult as spending our lives running from it. Embracing our vulnerabilities is risky but not nearly as dangerous as giving up on love and belonging and joy – the experiences that make us the most vulnerable. Only when we are brave enough to explore the darkness will we discover the infinite power of our light.
- Brene Brown

The **Life With Ziggy** project was never intended to become a book that I openly shared. Initially, my writings of Ziggy and our time together were just for me. The entries of my private journal were used to help document our recoveries and remind me of where we came from. As I slowly started sharing our story, I was encouraged by numerous supporters to share it more often. Their support led directly to the book you hold in your hands.

Depression, the disease, and the heinous toll it takes on millions of lives, was a driving force in urging me to take a step forward and share my secrets. Over time, I have realized that my bouts with depression, my attempts at suicide, and my recovery were necessities in my life. Without them, I wouldn't be the person I am today. Surviving my struggles provided me with a passionate desire to try to become a loving husband, patient father, grateful son, supportive brother, and playful uncle. I hope I am closer to being that person today.

While I was lucky enough to recover from the depression that once controlled my heart, it took years, just short of a decade, for me to fully accept myself and the things I had done. I still carry my scars, but they are constant reminders of the transformation that has occurred within me. I can look in the mirror, smile, and be grateful for the struggle that ultimately forever changed me.

In the eyes of man, I rescued Ziggy. In reality, Ziggy rescued me. I hold my memories of Ziggy very close to my heart. Even in death, my furry guardian angel provided me with a final opportunity to partake in his unique brand of therapeutic healing. Through the sharing of our story, he gave me a rare and priceless gift. This book marks a true achievement in my personal journey of recovery; to be able to share my story, my scars, and the darkest parts of me is the most difficult, and yet most therapeutic experience, I have ever had.

I am often asked if I regret the things that I did to myself. The question, while deeply personal, is very understandable. Unfortunately, I don't know how to answer that question. I regret a lot of things, but I know that if I were to take away parts of this section of my life, I would cease to be the person I am. I regret actions, emotions, and the fallout, but each part of it is part of me. It is who I have become. I will forever appreciate my scars, cherish my memories, and have gratitude for this struggle, because that is all I know how to do.

The insidiousness of depression doesn't discriminate. It does not selectively pick those it infects. It can infect anyone. If you are not the one suffering, you can almost guarantee that someone you know is. You may not know it, but statistics prove how widespread depression is. If you are suffering, please reach out to someone. I had countless people I could have confided in, but I chose to hide my pain. I buried my struggles, and that decision almost cost me my life.

I am lucky to be alive today, and I feel extremely blessed to be able to write these words. There are many more that have suffered, and they no longer have voices to share their stories. Without timely interventions in my life, the depression would have consumed me.

Hopefully, in some small way, the story of my struggle will help someone. Even if it is just one person, it is worth sharing the hardest parts of me; the ones that I kept hidden for so long.

Recovery, often seemingly impossible, can be a reality. It can happen, but it requires dedication, assistance, and time. It will not happen overnight, but if one reaches out for help, it can be a possibility. Recovery is the greatest gift that I have ever been given. Without it, I wouldn't have been able to marry my gorgeous wife, watch my twin sons come into the world, and spend every day savoring their unconditional love.

Recovery is a miracle. It lasts for a lifetime.
- Jackie Williams

In loving memory of Jamal and Ziggy;
the greatest friends a boy could ever have.

CONTENTS

CONTENTS

PART II: A DOG

CONTENTS

PART I: THE BOY

The best writing comes out when you find yourself broken. Your heart is ripped open and the feelings spill out into a beautiful mess on paper.

- Shannen Wrass

Chapter One: Is This The End...

In depression...faith in deliverance, in ultimate restoration, is absent. The pain is unrelenting, and what makes the condition intolerable is the foreknowledge that no remedy will come – not in a day, an hour, a month, or a minute. It is hopelessness even more than pain that crushes the soul.
- William Styron

I was awoken suddenly by the familiar sensation of a cold, wet nose pressed against my cheek. It was a comfortable feeling that I had become accustomed to over the past year. Every night I would be greeted by him in the same loving manner. The cold nose would always be paired with a warm kiss that would follow soon afterwards. But, for some reason, tonight was different.

He continued to nuzzle my cheek, pushing his snout firmly into me. I caressed his soft, floppy ear tenderly as I wiped the sleep from my tired eyes. He continued his dramatic urges, forcing me to sit up. I reached erratically towards the nightstand in an attempt to illuminate the room. As I did, he gingerly jumped off my bed, and headed towards his.

As the light engulfed the dark room, he glanced back at me with those big, dark, hopeful eyes, pausing for a second as he did, insisting that I follow. His actions were slow and disoriented. I trailed along behind him and watched his methodical movements. As he struggled to climb into his bed, tears filled my eyes. I lifted him softly and placed him on his pillow. He spun in a cautious circle and wearily dropped to his bed. He moaned feebly as he looked up at me with those eyes, still full of hope and love. They beckoned me, gesturing me to come closer.

I sat on his bed. He used what little energy he could muster to climb into my lap. He nudged my neck as I squeezed him close. Tears streamed down my cheeks and fell towards him. I cradled his head in my hands as he struggled to lift it. I nuzzled my face against his, and he slowly licked the tears from my cheeks. It was something he had done countless times before, but this time was different. I couldn't help but wonder if this was the end.

I thought about how we had gotten here. As the tears consumed my eyes, I thought about that fateful night almost two years ago. The night that brought us here, together, in this very moment...

My exhausted, bloodshot eyes gradually became consumed with tears as my once expressionless face was suddenly overcome by terror. My bright blue eyes had been radically transformed. The light that once resided in them had been replaced by an unmistakable sadness and a horrifying fear. Slowly, I brought a trembling hand to my dejected face and wiped a string of tears from my cheek.

The pale moonlight crept in through the small kitchen window, revealing the counter in front of me. As the dim light trickled in, the eerie scene became a little clearer. Sitting on the countertop, in front of my shaking body, sat the most horrific sight. The sight would become even more horrific once the realization of what had just transpired became a cognitive thought in my mind. The thought was difficult, painful, and even sickening to fathom. But, it was present nonetheless. Simply put, the thought was…"IS THIS THE END?"

It was a thought that had never entered my conscious mind before. In that moment, as I stood alone, it was suddenly the thought that consumed my brain. It was a thought that I had not been cognizant enough to understand. Maybe my pride had been masking the truth this entire time. Regardless, the evidence was damning. Still sitting on the counter on full display, basking in the moonlight, was evidence that I had a real problem. Each piece of it gawked back at me, trivializing my very existence. With a slight shrug and an unnerving smirk, each bottle snickered at my feelings of hopelessness and despair. Each one beckoned me, deceiving me, until it was too late. They had won.

Feelings of inadequacy overwhelmed me. Regret overpowered me. Depression and uncertainty incapacitated me. An intense, painful pressure resided in my chest as my heart pounded uncontrollably. I closed my weary eyes and let the darkness envelop me. There I stood, leaning against the cold kitchen counter, alone and scared. Outside, the winter night froze the Earth as tiny white snowflakes completed their methodical dance towards the ground. My heart sank at the realization that I couldn't even enjoy the falling of a snowflake anymore. The cold silence of the night turned the pits of my stomach. My hands trembled, my heart pounded, and my mind raced.

In that moment, as I stood there with the pale moonlight revealing the tragic scene, a flash flood of memories spilled into my brain. Each one appeared vividly in front of me. Each one was a simple reminder of the good stuff in life. Each one had shown itself just moments too late. With each memory, the tears began to flow more freely than ever before.

My knees buckled under the crushing weight of it all. The weight of my body seemed to have tripled. The devastating reality of my situation brought a powerful dizziness upon me. It sent my entire body spiraling towards the tile floor. In a desperate effort, I clawed at the slick countertop trying to restore my balance. Somehow, I managed to catch myself on the way down, but not before my head hit the countertop, and sent pills spilling everywhere.

The full winter moon was going to be the only keen observer of my demise. It was a saddening, but peaceful thought, to know that it would be the only one to see me at my weakest moment. Using the remaining strength I had left, I awkwardly straightened myself upwards. As I fought to stay on my feet, with a sweaty, shaking palm, I gently rubbed my forehead. The knot had already begun to form. I tried to shake the dizziness out of my head, but as my brain rattled, an indescribable pain consumed it.

Dazed and vaguely confused, I gazed down at the counter at the mess that I had just made. In my most fragile moment, as my life was slowly slipping away, the mess should have been the least of my worries. But, in that moment, I could only think about cleaning it up. It was not that the mess bothered me. It was the thought of my poor mother having to pick up after me that was too much to bear.

The thought of my mom brought frenzied sobs and a gushing of tears. Short gasps for breath were audible between furious shrieks of sadness and anger. I struggled to pick up the remaining pills. With each movement, my heart pounded harder. I had never felt anything like it. Was this how it was going to end?

The once full bottle of Benadryl was down to less than a half dozen. The newly opened bottle of Tylenol PM had been downed to less than half. The prescription bottles of Prozac and Lortab had been finished off. Bottles and caps sat haphazardly across the counter. My hands were shaking harder than ever as the cocktail of drugs made its way through my bloodstream. My heart continued to race causing an intense pain in my chest.

As the deadly mixture of pills surged through my system, I wondered just when my kidneys would fail. I pictured myself convulsing violently on the floor as my body shut down. My body would spasm uncontrollably for a few seconds before I finally rested. Maybe I would just quietly lose consciousness and slump to the floor. I really wasn't sure what would happen to me, but I knew the moon was in for a horrific show, and I was the unfortunate star.

My vision had begun to blur. I rubbed my eyes and blinked a couple times. I repeated the process, but no amount of rubbing or blinking was going to fix it. My depth perception was completely gone. I shook my head cruelly trying to rid myself of my infirmities, but it was to no avail. In fact, it only made things worse.

In a desperate effort to clean up, I frantically tried to grab one of the bottles in front me. I missed. I reached out and grasped wildly at the air to the left of the bottle, followed by a handful of counter to the right of it. Both times, I was positive that I was going to capture the menacing container but missed. Frustrated, I made one last attempt at snatching the bottle. As my fingers closed around it, I realized clearer than ever before what I had just done. I was going to die. The process had been put in motion, and I couldn't stop it. I was the architect of my own demise. I had just committed suicide.

Suicide. The word still didn't seem real. It was never a thought that lingered consciously in my mind. It had never been contemplated. It hadn't resided in my brain. It was never a passing thought. It hadn't been seriously considered. It hadn't even been joked about. It had never been a possibility. After all, it just didn't seem real. But, in less than two minutes of chaotic and mindless action, it became real. In minutes, it became my fate. And, in an instant, it was all going to end.

Just a couple of hours earlier, I had been holding this same bottle. It was a lot less menacing then. After tossing and turning for the majority of yet another sleepless night, I had gotten out of bed to take something to help me rest. After quickly downing a couple Tylenol PMs, I meandered back to the comfy confines of my bed. Two hours later, I was still tossing and turning. I was left staring at the ceiling fan, brewing in self-pity.

I wasn't really sure how I had gotten to this place, but the feelings of despair had tightened their grip. All I wanted was to sleep for a really long time. I wanted to forget about all the pain that resided in my heart. I just yearned for peace. I craved sleep. It seemed like a simple enough request, but for some reason, it wasn't being granted.

As the minutes turned into hours, I came to the conclusion that I was going to get some sleep. No matter what it took, I was going to close my eyes, and not wake up for a very long time. With my unwavering and stubborn mind set, I went back to the kitchen. I opened the cupboard and started searching for something to help my desire for sleep become a reality.

I cautiously, however, only took two more Tylenol PMs before I headed back to my bed. Once I was back to tossing and turning, my mind was once again bombarded by painful thoughts. I was so tired, and I desperately craved some relief. My head was pounding from the serious lack of sleep. My heart was broken and yearned for healing. Without thinking, I dragged myself out of bed once again.

I wondered why sleep hadn't come. For some reason, I couldn't control my thoughts. Each one weighed on me. Each one was the elephant in the room. I had a ton of them running rampart through my mind. I desired to share none of them, but for a moment, I wondered if talking about them would help. It didn't matter. Regardless of the answer, I was going to get some sleep.

As I approached the cupboard, I didn't know what I was about to do. There were no plans, no thoughts, and no emotions running through my troubled and tired mind. I felt as if I were outside of my body. I was in a daze, watching as my likeness grabbed medicine bottle after medicine bottle out of the cupboard. Over the counter and prescription drugs, it didn't matter. They were all lined up in front of me. They were all calling out to me. They were all promising the desperate relief that my heart yearned for.

I watched as a bottle of Benadryl was opened and quickly poured into my mouth. I gagged as the pills filled it. I dry-heaved violently as my body desperately strained to prohibit the massive quantity of pills from entering my system. I watched as my likeness grabbed a bottle of water from the fridge and gagged down all but six of the pills. The scene didn't stop there.

I continued to watch myself as the bottles of Tylenol PM, Lortab, and Prozac were opened and pills were consumed. I watched as some 205 odd pills were forced into my system. In mere seconds, I had consumed roughly 70 Benadryl's, 35 Tylenol PMs, 55 Prozacs, and 45 Lortabs. My system was flooded, and as I stood there minutes after taking them, I knew I was going to die.

As the snow slowly covered the Earth with a perfectly pure white blanket, I stood staring out the kitchen window on that cold January night, realizing my life was over. I wiped away the tears that continued to stream down my cheeks, stiffened my upper lip, and realized the coward that I had become. It is always those realizations that come far too late that are like punches to the gut. This realization was the hardest one yet. There was nothing left to do. I just needed to make my way to my room. I would finally be able to sleep, and my bed was calling my name.

I placed the bottles neatly back in the cupboard. My overwhelmed body suddenly felt like it was floating while being pounded by a jackhammer. My muscles were weak. Everything seemed so damn heavy. As I tried to take a small step, I realized my muscles were like Jell-O. My legs were dead weight, unable to fully support me. The weight of my legs, combined with their lack of stability, made it difficult to move. Slowly, I slid my weary feet across the tile floor attempting to escape from what I had just done.

The blurriness in my vision continued to get worse. The dizziness in my head was overpowering. Like a drunk, staggering down the alley, I made my way through the darkness. Angrily, I stumbled around, and I almost fell twice before I even made it out of the kitchen. My legs shook with each step. Weakness was consuming my body.

I no longer fully recognized who I was, or what I was doing. As I made it to the hallway, my knees buckled, and I collapsed. As I laid there, one thought crossed my mind; I didn't want to die here. But, I couldn't help but wonder if this was the end.

As I was sprawled out on the floor in the hallway, I began to choke as vomit started to force its way up. I forced it back down, and the sickening taste of acid resided in my throat. The burning sensation that consumed my esophagus was a repulsive reminder of what was happening to me. I covered my mouth with my hands and began to sob. I managed to muffle the sounds of my cries. More vomit began to come up, but once again, I forced it back down. My abdomen convulsed violently.

When the painful convulsing paused, I struggled to stand up. I immediately collapsed loudly back to the floor. Two more times, I attempted to get on my feet. The second time, I was only able to make it to my knees before falling hard back on my face.

I was too disoriented to stand and too weak to crawl. My heart had been pounding for too long. It was beginning to give up on me. I couldn't blame it. I had given up on myself. Paralyzed by fear and the clear realization that this was truly going to be the end, I pushed my face into the carpet and cried. I just cried...and cried...and cried.

As I sobbed, memories flooded into my mind. I thought about family and friends. I thought about loved ones. All of this just made the hysterical sobs worse.

I thought about my friends, and how they just wouldn't understand why. I thought about my family, and the pain this would cause them. I thought about my beautiful girlfriend, Meagan, and how this would break her heart. I thought about my selfishness. Lastly, I thought about my mom and dad finding my dead body in the hallway.

I thought about the screams of horror and the tears of despair. I thought about how they had never let me down, but in that moment, I would disappoint them more than ever before. I thought about my funeral, and the tears my mother would cry over me. I was a failure, a coward, and a quitter.

I was a letdown, a disappointment, a flop. Worthlessness overcame me. I looked over to the alcove where the washer and dryer sat as another horrific thought crossed my mind. How could I end this pain faster? The ruthlessness of depression was victorious, and I was done. I just wanted it to end.

As I laid weakly on the ground, I grasped at the base of the slider door and pushed it open. There, on the floor, within my reach, was a large bottle of Clorox Bleach. I stretched for it and grasped the handle. My mind was racing as a shaky hand unscrewed the lid. The overpowering stench of bleach filled the air. My eyes, already blurry and filled with tears, began to sting.

Tears ran uncontrollably down my cheeks. With my remaining strength, I lifted the bottle towards my mouth. As my lips touched the spout, I gagged. More sobs came as my body convulsed. I tried one more time, and as a small amount of bleach touched my tongue, I heaved. Disgustedly, I pushed the bleach back into the alcove. My sobbing increased as I struggled to close the simple slider door. Spent, I just laid there.

I pondered the thought of people knowing I was a coward. I contemplated the pain that this would cause my parents. With that in mind, I made a half conscious decision to try and survive. In a last ditch effort, I clawed at the carpet trying to pull myself along. I was only 25 feet from my parent's room. If only I could wake them. They could help me.

My mind was so tired. I couldn't keep my eyes open. I pulled myself hard, and I felt the carpet burns on my legs. My body dragged slowly across the floor with each strenuous pull.

I wasn't moving fast enough. I was inching along, getting weaker by the second. My mind was heavy and dizzy. The room was spinning all around me. I was beginning to pass out. Before I knew it, I lost consciousness right in front of my bedroom door. I was just twelve feet away from my parent's room. I was just twelve feet away from safety. Twelve feet was the difference between life and death. I was on the wrong side of the twelve feet.

A violent gag brought me back. An intense, bright light flashed in my eyes with each gag. My eyelids fluttered, but everything was so dark. I blinked, but my vision was still foggy.

I wasn't sure how long I had been out. It could have been just a couple minutes or a few hours. I tried to push my body upwards, but my hand was met by a small, wet pool. A sliver of light emanated from the tiny lamp in my bedroom, illuminating the vomit.

I tried to open my eyes wider and focus. My vision hadn't improved. It was much worse. Everything was so blurry. I could barely see things close to my face as my eyes tried to focus, but I could make out some shapes and shadows. I saw several pill casings in the midst of the vomit. I tried to scream, but the vomit in my throat muffled my words.

I didn't have any more energy to crawl. My body was spent. The poison was trying to shut my system down. I tried to yell again but only a whisper was released. It was over. It was time for me to accept it. I couldn't get up. I couldn't scream. I couldn't do anything. This was the end.

I used the final, dwindling strength I had left to pull myself the couple of feet inside my bedroom. I could not bear the thought of dying in the hallway. I didn't want my limp and lifeless body to be the first thing that they saw in the morning. I grabbed the picture of Meagan from my nightstand, and I clutched it in my hand. I couldn't see the picture as my vision was gone. I knew the picture though, and I could picture just how incredibly beautiful she looked. I thought about her long, silky brown hair. I pictured her hazel eyes that would look green in the sunlight. I imagined her little button nose and gorgeous lips. Tears poured out of the corners of my eyes as I thought about her warm, stunning smile. I thought about never holding her, never kissing her again. It was a realization that tormented my soul.

Still, the framed photo was comforting to hold in my hand. After the initial rush of emotion, it helped me calm down. My heart rate seemed to slow a little, and my chest didn't hurt as bad. I held the picture, and I spoke to her. In a dazed, muffled, slurred voice, I told her that I was sorry, and that I would always love her. I brought the picture to my lips and kissed it. I imagined I was kissing her soft lips one last time. For a moment, I felt happy.

She had been my happiness for the past eight months. A happiness that I had taken for granted. I didn't deserve her anyway. I was a coward, and she deserved more than a lowly coward. Then, before another thought came into my mind, I let go. There, on my bedroom floor, I stayed. I didn't move. The lights had gone out, and no one was home.

That's the thing about depression: A human being can survive almost anything, as long as she (he) sees the end in sight. But depression is so insidious, and it compounds daily, that it's impossible to ever see the end.
- Elizabeth Wurtzel

Chapter Two: Into Hell...

Sometimes I wonder if suicides aren't in fact
sad guardians of the meaning of life.
- Vaclav Havel

Luck. I had never been a firm believer in it. Four leaf clovers, the foot of a rabbit, and horseshoes were never in my possession. I had never gone around thinking any particular person was lucky or unlucky. I had never been superstitious, at least, not since the last time I listened to Stevie Wonder. I always thought that things happened for a reason. We weren't always sure what the reason was, but they happened for one all the same.

I believed that it was human nature to discover one's true self during the hardest, darkest, and most hopeless times. I thought that the chaos of a difficult situation helped trigger growth and development, which led to a better, more well-rounded human being. Still, I knew that human nature was, and still is, to equate the outcome of a chaotic situation to luck. Since I have never been a firm believer in luck, where did that put me? My ticket wasn't in the "luck" sweepstakes, nor had it been for a very long time.

As things sat now, luck couldn't hurt. I needed some luck, and I needed it quick. Incapacitated on my bedroom floor, passed out in my own vomit, I could use any sort of luck, or grace, or divine intervention available. I could have used any assistance, because as it was, I was screwed. I couldn't help myself at all. It was only a matter of time before death reached out its cold hand and took me with it.

I was on Hell's doorstep, and the Devil was beckoning me to come in from the cold. His fires blazed, and I could feel the intense heat radiating from his direction. The Grim Reaper sat eerily on his side, with his outstretched, bony finger pointed in my direction.

Hell's minions had surrounded me, making retreat impossible. In my despair and self-pity, I ended up right where Satan wanted me. Vulnerable, full of self-loathing, distraught and embarrassed, he had helped to create the coward that now sat in front of him. He was pleased. His sinister grin terrified me as it captured my eyes. Involuntarily, I crawled towards my captors as the minions nipped at my heels. Hell was going to become my home.

The thought of eternal damnation and endless suffering had never crossed my mind before. Now, that thought crippled me, paralyzing my soul. A little while earlier, however, it probably would've seemed like a welcomed relief. Still, the thoughts of disappointing my mom and dad seemed more devastating than the fires, the horns, and the pitchforks of my future.

The Grim Reaper reached out and grasped my neck as Satan laughed. It was over. I was finished. My suicide was complete.

My body convulsed and shook me from the Reaper's grasp. I gagged violently, as my body attempted to rid itself of the poison coursing through my system. My head jerked, and I came to as I vomited on the floor. I felt the jagged edges of pill casings in my throat and mouth. Their pointy ends cut my esophagus and tongue. The texture of them made me gag again, and more vomit spilled out of my mouth. My stomach contracted painfully with each convulsion.

My vision was still blurred, but I could make out pink, brown, blue, and white pills in the vomit. Some were just the outer pill casings, and others, were pills that hadn't completely broken down yet. Maybe there was some hope after all.

As I saw the casings, I was again reminded of my stupidity. I tried to yell, but I was unable to let out much more than a weak moan. My brain was not allowing me to think. It would not allow me to function. I could not stay awake.

The feelings of helplessness and inadequacy that had helped to land me in this situation were returning. Shortly after I had come to, I was back out. Over the next few minutes, this would happen over and over again, as my body was trying to reject the poison I had provided it. It was slowly losing the battle though. My system was on overload, and the shutting down process had begun. It was only a matter of time. Soon, it was all going to end...

Convulse. Vomit. Consciousness. Vomit. Yell. Lose consciousness.

The pattern could have continued for minutes or hours. I really had no time frame to reference the entire situation. Before I lost consciousness again, I grabbed the journal that sat on my nightstand. The smooth leather felt soft in my hand. The touch of the journal brought back a memory of birthday cake and presents. It wasn't a memory I wanted to have. Not now. Not like this.

Tears streamed. With chicken-scratch, I attempted to write what I thought was the word "Sorry". It was one of the most frustrating experiences of my life. I couldn't even write the word "Sorry" on my own. I struggled to see. I struggled to hold my head up. I struggled to use my muscles. The pen fell from my hand as I struggled to stay conscious. Before I could finish, I passed out, again.

I awoke in a beautiful dream. I saw flickers of bright, colorful lights. They danced around my mind, each one providing a beautiful backdrop for a memory. I saw flashes of family and friends. Memories came flooding into my mind, each one joining the colors in their methodical, rhythmic dance. My neurons were firing in all directions. Memory after memory sped along my information highway. Thought after thought jumped from synapse to synapse at an incredible rate. My brain was firing in all directions. A jumble of memories and thoughts shot off in my head. I couldn't keep up with all of them.

A Michael Jordan jumper, Meagan's smile, my pops cheering, a homecoming dance, Bob Marley lyrics, a Cross Country State Championship, a day at the lake, my mom baking cookies, a basketball game, Christmas morning 1996, high school graduation. It was all there, one after another. Each one sped off as soon as it came, until one stuck.

A memory of my dad yelling my name came to the forefront of my senses. It was fuzzy though. It wasn't as sharp as the rest. But, it was there. My dad was yelling my name. It may have been at a basketball game, a cross country race, or at a family BBQ. I couldn't really tell. All I kept hearing was "JAMMER! JAMMER! JUSTIN! JUSTIN DALE!" It happened over and over again. I couldn't make out where we were at. I wanted to call out to him, but I couldn't talk. In my memory, I just stared into the blurry abyss as he continued to yell.

At first, his voice seemed to be cheerful. It was as if he were urging me on. I must have been running in an important cross country race or playing in a big time basketball game. He was cheering for me to do my best. After a couple of times screeching, "JAMMER! JAMMER! JUSTIN! JUSTIN DALE!" his voice seemed to be overcome with panic. The cheering had suddenly subsided. It was replaced by an eerie, horrific, screaming voice. It was a voice filled with doubt, fear, panic, and uncertainty. His tone absolutely terrified me, rocking me to my core.

My dream was interrupted. Suddenly, my body shook violently, and I felt a firm pat on my cheek. Had I really been dreaming? Was this real? The voice of my father returned to the forefront of my senses.

"JAMMER! JAMMER! JUSTIN! JUSTIN DALE! DAMMIT! WHAT IN THE HELL DID YOU DO?!! JAMMER! PLEASE NO!"

The voice was muffled. It sounded so very far away. Was it coming from another room? Maybe I was underwater. I couldn't tell. Still, one thing was unmistakable, the voice sounded absolutely horrified.

My body shook hard yet again. I felt a slap on my cheek. It was much harder than the previous pat. My cheek began to sting. My eyelids fluttered, and a flicker of bright light shot through. I opened my heavy eyes, but everything was still a blur. I could, however, see a shadow moving around. The movements were quick, fluid, and with purpose. The shadow dashed here and then there. As my eyes opened wider, the blurry figure came more into view. For a moment, it scared me. I wasn't sure who or what it was.

The shadow came closer, and the panicked voice returned. The voice was now clearer than ever before. This time, it was unmistakable. Despite the panic, I could make out the voice of my dad. And, this time, I could make out the figure. Through the fog, I could make out the kind, concerned face of my pops. I rubbed at my eyes. He looked down at me as he cradled my head in his hands. He had tears in his eyes. I couldn't understand why the tears were there. But, as I began to vomit again, I turned my head to the side, and my eyes glimpsed a pile of pill casings on the floor. In that moment, I realized just why the tears were there.

As I began to comprehend that realization, tears filled my eyes. My brain was racing, but I still couldn't speak. For a small moment, I thought about my dad watching me die. I thought about dying in his arms, and the endless torment racked my soul with that thought. I thought about him holding my limp body as it took its last breath. It was a heart-wrenching combination of thoughts. They were thoughts that brought pain to my heart and tears to my eyes. Worst of all, I thought once again about the coward I had become, the coward that my dad now knew I was. It ripped my heart out. I could see the pain, the confusion, the anger, and the desperation in his face. More than that, through the fog that covered my eyes, I thought I could see disappointment. More than anything, that look crumbled my already broken heart.

He shouted to me again, and this time, I felt like I understood. My brain was still a mess of thoughts. My head was still pounding and filled with an uncontrollable pain. Through it all, I still understood him. My eyes were heavy, and they refused to stay open. He was trying desperately to keep me awake. I fought to keep them open as he pushed me towards consciousness. He shouted again...

"JAMMER! JAMMER! What did you do? What did you take?"

I tried to answer, but my throat was dry and painful. I tried to swallow, but there was no saliva in my mouth. My throat was raw and irritated. Pain came with each attempt. My mouth tasted like acid. The residing taste of the vomit was horrible, and it was a constant reminder of the state I was in.

The terrifying darkness began to envelop me again. My eyes fluttered. My head was heavy, too heavy for me to hold up. Even as it lay cradled in my father's hands, the weight was overwhelming. Everything was a blur. I lost consciousness again. My body went limp as my brain tried to shut off. In that moment, I thought I had just died in my father's arms. The thought sent horrific chills down my spine. The chaos was concluding. It was over.

I was in and out of consciousness. While conscious, my neurons were firing in every direction. I held conversations with people who were not present; I shared memories from the past, and I spoke gibberish while laughing at my own jokes. My dad tried to keep me lucid, but it was to no avail. I was fried, with no idea of what was happening in the real world. I was lost, wandering around in the corners of my mind. At one point, I asked someone why I had to hate myself. And, I cried.

I was loaded into the backseat of my parent's car. It would take too long for an ambulance to get to me, so they had to rush me to the hospital. My thought was "Why bother?" I was going to die anyways. It was over. After seeing the fear and sadness in the eyes of my parents, I felt like I wanted to die. I didn't think I could face them. Despite their unconditional love, the devastation, confusion, and sorrow that was present on their faces was like a million arrows piercing my already tattered heart. I was forever stained. I was permanently broken.

As the car flew down the highway, I continued my discussions with people who weren't around. I proceeded to share memories of anything and everything that came to my mind. I shared basketball stats with my dad, song lyrics with my mom, and the Periodic Table with Albert Einstein.

I was so far out of it that I struggled to comprehend what was happening. By now, the poison had made itself at home. Its overwhelming power was in full swing, and I no longer had any idea where I was, or what was going on. Then, I was unconscious for quite some time. I would come back, but I wasn't able to stay conscious for long. The drugs were working their magic, and it wasn't looking good.

I was rushed into the emergency room as I regained consciousness. My actions were labeled as a suicide attempt. There was that word again…suicide. I really wasn't sure why it was being thrown around. I just wanted some sleep. But, with the desire for sleep came an overdose. There I was, in the emergency room, labeled as what sounded like a junkie. I was just a junkie who overdosed while trying to commit suicide. Could I get anything right? For a moment, I thought the only thing I would ever get right was the suicide. My only real achievement would be the successful suicide that I hadn't really meant to attempt. I was a failure.

How did I get here? How in the hell did I end up here? What had happened to me? Despite all the chaos that had consumed the past few hours, I had been able to think. I had been able to contemplate on my situation. Though my brain was foggy, I understood much of what had happened. I still wasn't sure why it happened. But, nonetheless, it did.

On the surface, I was loopy, drugged, and disoriented. Underneath, my mind was racing, and some cognitive thought was present. I felt regret and pain. I felt despair and hopelessness. It was all running through my head. I laid in the hospital bed, slightly dazed, and more than a little confused.

I fought to keep my eyes open as the nurses rushed around me. They pulled me upwards and into a sitting position. As they did, the dizziness in my head got worse. A bucket was thrust into my lap as I began to dry heave. My stomach was turning. Acid began to rise in my esophagus. I forced it back down as a nurse placed a paper cup to my lips. The substance inside the cup was thick and black.

What was this? Why did I need to drink it? It looked and smelt like tar. I was confused. Fear consumed me. I panicked and purged my lips. I shook my head, refusing to take a drink. Where was I? Why was I here? What was going on? A second time, the cup was put to my lips, and I refused. I was in panic mode. Were these nurses trying to kill me? It didn't matter anyways. I was already dying. It was only a matter of time.

Finally, I gave in. I slowly partook of the thick, black substance. It was activated charcoal. It was disgusting. Slowly, with help from the nurses, I gagged it all down. It slid down my raw throat, and I felt the grittiness as it did. It was sickening. It was the worst taste I had ever experienced.

Immediately after, a cup of pills was thrust in front of me. The small assortment of pills was needed to slow down my heart rate and start my digestive processes on the right track. I couldn't even look at them. Every time they caught my glancing eyes, I was reminded of the some 205 odd pills that were running rampant through my system. The poison of each one was coursing through my veins. I was reminded of the feeling of 50 pills in my mouth. I was reminded of collapsing in the hallway. I was reminded of vomit. I was reminded that I was a coward. I was reminded that I was going to die.

I believed my life was over. It was over, and I was going to spend my final moments in a hospital bed, drinking charcoal shakes, and being terrified of pills. The cup of pills frightened me, but I took them all the same. The texture of the pills brought back horrifying memories of the previous hours. It was again a reminder of the shame I was feeling. I wondered when I would die, so this would all go away.

My heart rate began to slow, and my body started to relax. For the past few hours, my system had been in a constant state of shock. My heart had pounded harder than ever before. The pains had been unbearable as my heart tried to crawl out of my chest. But, finally, I was able to relax. As I did, my eyes started to close. My body went limp, and I was either passed out, fast asleep, or dead.

The chaos of the past few hours was only the beginning. I had faced the Grim Reaper, and I looked right into his cold, dark eyes. I had watched myself reach the lowest point possible. I had watched myself nearly die. I had been into Hell. Only one question remained...could I make it back out?

Depression is such a cruel punishment. There are no fevers, no rashes, no blood test to send people scurrying in concern, just the slow erosion of self, as insidious as cancer. And like cancer, it is essentially a solitary experience; a room in hell with only your name on the door.
- Martha Manning

Chapter Three: Afraid of Hope...

Depression is a flaw in chemistry not character.
- Unknown

Nervous and scared, I began to wander aimlessly through the darkness. Fear griped me at every turn. My heart pounded in anticipation. I waited for the Grim Reaper to magically appear in front of me. The fogginess was beginning to subside, and as I walked, the mist began to recede. In the distance, I could see a tiny sliver of light piercing the empty blackness. Cautiously, I limped along in the direction of the light. Through the pain, through the regret, and through the uncertainty, I trudged forward. The light was getting closer, and I began to feel hope.

Hope. These feelings were new. I hadn't felt hopeful for a very long time. Like luck, hope wasn't something that I ever really concerned myself with. Up to this point in my life, I hadn't ever seriously needed to hope for anything. My hopes consisted of video games, basketball shoes, and other material goods. They were really wants, not hopes.

I grew up in a middle class family. My parents worked extremely hard to provide for our family. They sacrificed so we could have the things we wanted. We never went without the things we needed. For the majority of my life, I had wants...not hopes.

When I started to feel hope, however, it came from a deep desire to be healed. I begged, pleaded, and prayed for healing. I yearned for it. I wished for it. And, yes...I hoped for it. When it refused to come, I gave up on it. After all, hope, like luck didn't seem to make much sense. By my senior year in high school, I stopped hoping for much of anything.

In time, I became afraid of hope. It was a constant reminder of a failure. A recap of mounting disappoint and insurmountable pain. It was a source of heartbreak. Why hope for things that were never going to come true? I never really wanted to set myself up for heartbreak from the beginning. So, eventually, the idea of hope simply disappeared. As quickly as it had appeared, it left.

Throughout my life, I had experienced my share of health problems. I fought. I struggled. While I had never faced cancer or fought some rare life-threatening disease, I slowly writhed. I hurt. And, I had almost died. Every single person experiences different struggles and challenges throughout his/her life. Some people have the ability to overcome more than others. We all struggle and are challenged on varying levels. I never sought to compare my adversities with those of others.

Some have looked at my challenges and considered me weak. No one will know the things I experienced. No one will know the exact things I suffered. No one walked in my shoes. No one will fully understand or know the physical, mental, and emotional scars that I carry.

No one but my Savior, Jesus Christ, has or ever will experience the exact pains I did. He is the only one that will have a perfect understanding of my trials. Similarly, I will never truly experience anyone else's pain and suffering. Because of that, I have never compared the struggles of one person to another. It just didn't seem right. My struggles were my own, and theirs belonged to them.

When I was five years old, I almost died. As a child, my body was attacked by a parasite called giardia. It ravaged my system for two years. I lost weight, lost energy, and tried not to lose hope. Luckily, I was little enough to not truly understand or comprehend the situation. Doctor's visits, needles, and fevers were a normal part of my life. My parent's tried to shield me from the pain, but it was impossible. The tests were never ending, and the effort to save my life was looking to be a failure.

At one point, the doctors told my mom to take me home and just spend time with me, because I was going to die. There was nothing left that they could do. They had no idea what was plaguing my body, and I was better off spending my last hours at home with family. That night my fever spiked, my eyes rolled back in my head, and my parents braced themselves for my untimely passing. Somehow, prayers were answered, and I was spared. I had survived. Maybe, just maybe, hope was real. Or, at the very least, the hope of others was real.

A couple days after the doctors had sent me home to die, they called my parents. They knew what I had, they knew how to cure it, and within weeks I would be as good as new. It was true. It worked. I was cured. I had hope.

In junior high, I started to feel sick again. It happened more often than not. I would shake. I would feel worn down. I would get weak. I would vomit. It affected me in the classroom, on the basketball court, and with my friends. After months of feeling this way, I was finally tested for diabetes. My health history made me a prime candidate to be attacked by the disease.

My memories of the testing for diabetes are probably much worse than the actual test really is. But, due to my history with needles, I was terrified. Fasting, drinking glucose, and needles did not mix well for me. In the end, I was diagnosed with hypoglycemia. I was a borderline diabetic, and if I didn't take care of myself, the disease would come for me.

With subtle and small changes in my lifestyle, I got back to feeling good again. I was fixed. I had hope.

In high school, I was a great student, a decent athlete, and had my share of great friends. I excelled in school, graduating 7th in my class, with only two B's my Freshman year that kept me from standing on the podium and addressing my classmates. I was in National Honor Society, Student Council, and Letterman's Club. I was the Homecoming King. I was an Eagle Scout. I participated in cross country, basketball, and track. I was an all-state athlete, held school and zone records, and won state championships with my buddies.

Life was good. I dated pretty girls, stayed clean from drugs and alcohol, and worked a fun job in the summers. There was nothing, in my mind, to complain about. I am sure that didn't keep me from complaining about something, but I really had no complaints.

When my senior year of high school rolled around, I was already a two-time state champion and an all-state athlete, held school records in track relays, and was the starting point guard on the varsity basketball team. After a successful senior season in cross country, where I ran to a fourth place finish at the state championships, basketball began. Early on in the season, I suffered a very serious concussion. While attempting a lay-up on a fast break, another player undercut me, and my body immediately inverted and went flying to the floor. I landed squarely on my head.

After somehow getting home, I was delusional. I couldn't remember where my room was. I began to vomit, and I ended up in the intensive care unit. I was dehydrated, and scared as the nurse tried desperately to insert an IV. Each needle bent in my arm. In the end, it took three nurses and ten needles to finally get a viable IV in my hand. My love for needles only grew. While in the ICU, the doctors were concerned about the possibility of severe bleeding in my brain. After a week in ICU and countless tests, I was finally released. The injury knocked me out of school for over a month.

The concussion caused very serious issues with my brain. Suddenly, I wasn't producing enough serotonin. My happy juice wasn't working properly, and it was only a matter of time before it caught up with me. Constant, painful, crippling migraines followed for months after the accident. Even years later, I still regularly suffered from them. Regardless of the headaches, it was the missing of the majority of my senior basketball season that really crushed me. I lost hope.

As track season started, I began suffering from severe stomach issues. The pain and nausea caused me to quit running. Every time I was active, I would vomit. I spent weeks in the hospital as doctors tried to discover my illness. I was tested for Leukemia, Crohn's disease, ulcers, appendicitis and anything else you can think of. Hospital visits became routine as doctor after doctor failed to figure out what was attacking my body. With each referral, each test, and each confused diagnosis, I began to lose any hope that I had left. I was no longer afraid of hope, instead I just let go of it.

Frustration led to sadness as appointment after appointment led to me giving up. I simply stopped caring about getting better. I felt like no relief would ever come. I believed that hoping for healing caused more heartache than it was really worth. I let self-pity begin to take over.

A year after I graduated high school, at 19 years old, I had dropped 20 pounds. Being a slender athlete my entire life, I didn't have any extra pounds to lose. I went from approximately 150 pounds to 130 pounds in less than a year. I would vomit on a daily basis, and I never felt quite right.

I spent increasingly less time running, playing basketball, and hanging out with friends. I found myself spending more time alone in my room playing video games, watching movies, and writing. I struggled to sleep. I was as pale as a ghost, with eyes as black as coal to boot. I began to look like a suffering shell of my former self. As the depression slowly started to enslave me, I felt powerless. Still, I concealed it. I hid the depression. I hoped.

I hoped for it to all go away.

As the depression worsened, I learned to mask my true emotions. On the outside, I would smile, joke, and laugh. On the inside, I was dying. I gave up on trying new things, or finding happiness in the smallest, or most unlikely of places. I stepped away from activities, places, and people I once enjoyed.

All the warning signs were there, but it wasn't until I was deemed too sick to serve my LDS mission to Atlanta, Georgia, that the true depression began to rear its ugly head. I still kept it hidden, but it slowly began to take over my life.

I had always wanted to serve a mission. I remembered singing "I Hope They Call Me on a Mission" in Sunday school. I remembered asking my uncle about his mission and writing my brother letters while he served his. I wanted the experience. The experience was suddenly taken from me, and I couldn't understand why.

Young men in the Church of Jesus Christ of Latter Day Saints (Mormons) are strongly encouraged to serve a mission. For me, that strong encouragement led to expectation. Expectation led to pressure. The pressure to be a missionary was simply overwhelming. I felt pulled in every direction. I felt eyes on me. I was questioned about why I wasn't serving, and the rumors began. It quickly became too much for me. Suddenly, I hated going to church, and I hated myself.

My parents never told me that I had to go on a mission. They never said they would love me less if I didn't. But, a deep part of me felt like they would. I felt like family and friends expected me to serve, regardless of whether I was physically able to do so or not. I felt like people just wouldn't understand why I wasn't serving. In reality, I put all the pressure and expectations on myself. It all quickly became too much for me to overcome.

I began to question myself. I began to question God. Why had He taken away my opportunity to serve? I wondered why He chose to take away my opportunity to serve rather than my illness. I began to lose faith. I had been sick for so long, and I wasn't getting better. I started on a downward spiral of self-loathing, disappointment, and despair.

Still, there is much more to my story, but it is far more then I want to share. There was Jamal, who I utterly refuse to talk or write about in public. I keep my thoughts of him in my head and my feelings in my heart. I always will. My experiences with him changed my life. But, his untimely passing caused more resentment. The pain accelerated my downward spiral. That tragic, out of control, downward spiral almost ended my life. It had landed me in here, fighting for my life.

My eyes opened slowly, gradually adjusted to the dim light. I blinked a couple of times. I had no idea where I was, or how long I had been there. I heard the beeping of a machine, and I felt a cuff tighten on my arm and then release. My nose tickled, and my hand ached. I reached upwards to my face with the aching hand and felt a tug. I felt a tube running along my face just below my nose. I felt an IV in my hand. As the fogginess in my mind began to subside, I realized why I was there.

I was alive. I had survived. I was not sure how I felt about it. As I continued the process of waking up, I felt a hand on my shoulder. I turned my head to see my dad, with tears in his eyes, smiling at me. I couldn't bring myself to smile back.

I was ashamed. Tears filled my eyes as I looked away. He just squeezed my shoulder, and we both cried. For some time, I covered my face and sobbed. I buried my ashamed head. The palms of my hands filled with a flooding of my tears. His hand squeezed my shoulder tighter as he pulled me into his arms. As he did, my sobs came in loud, painful gasps. With each one, he just held me tighter. I was ashamed. I was confused. I was heartbroken. I was scared. I knew he was disappointed. But, I knew he loved me, and I was alive.

Before we could discuss the night's events, a slew of nurses came rushing in. One jammed a needle in my arm and took some blood, another changed my IV bag, and the last one updated my chart while we waited for the doctor. My head still pounded, and my eyes burned from the tears I had cried. Unfortunately, it was only the beginning. The floodgates opened, and I wept uncontrollably.

I tried to compose myself, but I was overcome with emotion. As the doctor spoke to my parents, I couldn't help but wonder what was being said about me. I couldn't help but wonder what was going to happen to me. I knew I had a serious problem, and I needed help. I didn't want to accept that fact, but I couldn't hide from it for long. If I wanted to survive, I had to accept help.

Maybe, for a moment, I would let myself hope. After all, somehow I was still alive after the chaos of the night. Maybe, things really did happen for a reason. Maybe, no matter how bad things are, there is always room for that small glimmer of hope.

Isn't it the moment of the most profound doubt that gives birth to new certainties? Perhaps hopelessness is the very soil that nourishes human hope; perhaps one could never find a sense of life without first experiencing its absurdity.
- Vaclav Havel

Chapter Four: Uncertainties...

People are supposed to fear the unknown, but ignorance is bliss
when knowledge is so damn frightening.
- Laurell K. Hamilton

I was embarrassed. I was ashamed. I was disappointed. I had permanent scars, and I was scared. But, I was alive. ALIVE! For a moment, that word took on new meaning. For a moment, that word meant hope. HOPE! That wasn't something that I had felt in a long time. Still, I was terrified of what the future held.

The growing uncertainty that I was feeling was clawing at me. It tore at my insides. It was weighing me down, more and more, every single day. That was how I ended up here. I let doubt get the best of me. I had let depression overcome me. I had let my feelings of inadequacy, fear, worthlessness, and utter despair consume me. The depression was so insidious, so utterly heartbreaking, that the depths of sorrow were literally feasting on my brittle and broken soul.

Those thoughts were difficult to swallow. I had fallen down hard, and it was time to get back up. I couldn't let the feelings of inadequacy consume me. Still, it was tough for me to stand after all that had happened, both literally and figuratively. It was going to be tough for quite a while, but I knew the sooner that I did it, the better off I would be.

The cuff tightened on my arm, and it interrupted my thoughts. My vision was still blurry from the tears that continued to consume my eyes. I blinked, trying to help them on their journey. Slowly, they would run down my cheeks making their desperate escape. I watched as a doctor escorted my parents back into the room. I couldn't look them in their eyes. I stared downwards, listening as the doctor spoke.

My eyes drifted upwards from time to time, but they never lingered there for long. I had hurt a lot of people, and I was realizing that more than ever now. My heart began to break as I thought of each person, one by one. The doctor's words were no longer ringing in my ears as faces of family and friends flashed before my eyes. Each one, I hoped would find it in their heart to forgive me. And, maybe one day, I would be able to look each one of them in their eyes again.

I thought about the time I had lied about the D+ that I had gotten on my math test. I couldn't look my parents in their eyes then. An attempt to end your life is a little more serious than lying about your math test. If I couldn't do it then, how was I ever going to look them in the eyes now?

"Is that alright Justin?" The doctor's soothing voice had broken the daze I was in. I had no idea what had been said amongst them as I day dreamed. I had been too busy rehashing the past, and fearing the future, to listen. He repeated himself a little louder, "Justin, you will spend a couple days in a rehab facility, is that alright? They will get you the help that you need."

I always wondered why he asked me if it was alright. It wasn't like I was allowed to say "No", although I really wanted to. I really didn't have a choice though. I could talk and talk, but it would go in one ear and out the other. To them, I was a threat to myself. I was mentally ill, and I was in severe need of professional psychiatric help. I needed to be locked up, watched after, at least for a little while. But, I just wanted to go home, and go back to sleep. I knew I needed help, but I didn't want it. I wasn't ready to accept the instability of my situation. I wasn't ready for what was to come.

I no longer recognized myself. I didn't know who I was, or what I wanted. I didn't think I had wanted to die. I didn't think I had wanted to hurt myself. I didn't want to think that I was depressed or suicidal. All the thoughts that were running through my head confused me. So, for a while, I just closed my eyes and tuned out the discussion around me. I pretended that I was on a beach. The soothing sound of the ocean's waves calmed me. A cool breeze brushed against my cheek. In that split second, I was relaxed. I was in paradise.

Quickly though, my paradise began to fade, and I started to shake. Just as quickly as I had made it appear, it left. My stomach growled as it turned. Nervously, I shut my eyes tighter. Maybe, I thought, just maybe...if I closed my eyes tight enough that I could make myself end up on the beach again. I wanted to be back in that paradise, but paradise was gone. It was replaced by bare walls, the beeping of a heart monitor, and a musty smell, mixed with latex.

The gurney that supported my weak and tired body began to move. As it approached a set of double doors, it came to a halt. My father stood there. He squeezed my hand, and I saw tears in his eyes. My mother stood next to him, tears streaming down her face. My fragile heart broke all over again. Each of their tears was a tragic reminder of the crossroads I was facing. I closed my eyes as tears consumed them. I couldn't look at the worry that devoured the faces of those two wonderful people who loved me with all their hearts.

Few words were spoken. Fewer looks were shared. They didn't have to be. A squeeze of the hand, a caress of a cheek, and a pat on the head...each one conveyed a loving message of support. Each was a message that I wasn't ready for. Each was a message that wasn't deserved. Each was a message that I desperately needed.

As the gurney was pushed through set after set of doors, my thoughts were racing. Where was I going? Why did I have to go there? Why couldn't I just go home? Anxiety was beating at my chest. Like a child, I wished for the safety of my own home. I just wanted to cuddle up in my own bed. As I was longing for a sense of normalcy, I was shook from my thoughts. The gurney slammed through the final set of double doors, and I was thrust out into the world.

The sun was still shining. I wasn't sure how that was possible. Just moments earlier, the darkness was all-consuming. It was an eerily cold morning, but the sunlight remedied that some. As I closed my eyes, and breathed in fresh air, my mind began to wander. Suddenly, a moment of panic overcame me, and I jolted upwards. I flailed my head around in every direction. I didn't want anyone to see me like this.

For some incomprehensible reason, I felt like everyone was watching me. If they hadn't been, my uncontrollable flailing surely would have signaled them to look my way. Still, I couldn't stop. I wasn't sure why this was occurring, but it was. The paramedics scrambled to my side. They grabbed my arms and pushed them down to my sides. I felt a hand on my chest as they urged my tense body back to the safety of the gurney. Shaking. Trembling. Scared. I laid there.

As tears once again filled my swollen, tired eyes, I thought about all that was happening. I couldn't comprehend why all this was happening. I couldn't understand how I had gotten here. It was surreal and scary. As my arms were cinched down, I felt helpless. The despair was returning. It was a good thing that I was strapped down to the gurney, because I wasn't sure what I might do.

I found myself wishing I had succeeded in the suicide attempt that I hadn't meant to attempt. I found myself seeing my coffin, my funeral, and my gravestone. I found myself wishing I was dead.

I was loaded into the ambulance with a loud thud. I closed my painful eyes as tightly as I could. Tears trickled slowly from their corners, escaping from the darkness that once held them. My mind wandered incessantly. Through the pounding in my weary head, I thought about where I was headed. In reality, I wasn't really sure. I didn't listen to the doctor. I couldn't bring myself to. I didn't want to discuss last night's fiasco. All I knew was that I was going to a mental hospital, and I guess I needed it.

The paramedic sat cautiously beside me. The smell of latex consumed the cabin. I glanced around at all the equipment as I thought about how cool this ride would have been ten years ago and under different circumstances. There was that time in kindergarten or first grade that I ran into that yellow cement pole while playing tag. The mammoth welt on my head grew by the second, but I hadn't needed an ambulance then. It sure would have been pretty awesome if I had needed one that day. I would have been the talk of my class and, despite those circumstances, I would have been happy with the ride. Now was different though. It wasn't nearly as cool.

The paramedic was an older gentleman with short gray hair. As he stared down at me, he appeared to have some glorious insight that he wanted to share. He said nothing, but I could tell he was thinking something. He looked at me so intently that I felt his gaze in my chest. His green eyes peered over his glasses, and he finally smiled. He clearly knew where I was headed. I wasn't sure if it was a courtesy smile or a smile of true concern. Either way, it didn't really matter. I wasn't ready for smiles of true concern, and I was expecting a great deal of courtesy smiles in the coming hours, days, weeks, and months.

As he continued to look my way, he took his hand, and rubbed his goatee that was also starting to gray. Small tears still slowly trickled from my eyes. I couldn't stand it any longer. The looks, the smiles, the judgment...I hated it all. Finally, I asked him.

"What? What do you have to say? Want to know why?"

Wide-eyed, he looked at me and set his jaw hard. He closed his green eyes as he responded to my inquiry. His response surprised me. He calmly patted my shoulder and smiled. "Son," he said "Why is not a question I have nor is it one that you probably want to discuss right now. I just want you to know that I can tell your parents truly love you. I could tell by the way they looked at you as you laid there. Just know that...ok?"

The comments didn't help relieve the tears. Rather, the floodgates opened up. These comments were not any great revelation to me. I already knew this, but to hear it from someone else, a complete stranger, hit me a little harder.

I didn't say anything. No response would do justice to the comment he shared, so I just looked away. What could I say? I had put myself here, and I had hurt a lot of people in the process. Those people really cared about me. They had watched me grow up from a pain in the ass toddler, to a pain in the ass teenager. They had sat in the stands at my basketball games, cross country meets, and scout ceremonies. They were people who loved me. Few of them actually knew the real me though. Hell, I didn't know the real me.

Self-loathing and disappointment prevented me from understanding just how any of those people could care about me, let alone love me. I just didn't understand, so I pondered that question as the ambulance made its way to the University Neuropsychiatric Institute located in Salt Lake City at the University of Utah.

It was ironic. At points in my life, I had desired to attend the University of Utah. My dad loved the Utes and had spent time there. He could often be seen in his red U of U hat. Now, I was going there, but it was neither under the circumstances, nor section of the University that I desired. It wasn't why, or how, I wanted to end up there. But, it was going to happen anyway.

During the ride, regardless of my previous thoughts, a sense of calming peace overcame me. For the first time in about 20 hours, I was beginning to relax. I wasn't sure if it was because of the comments of the paramedic, or the fact that I wouldn't have to face anyone who knew me for a little while. Whatever it was, I liked it. I enjoyed the calmness for as long as I could.

It was short lived however. As the vehicle came to an abrupt stop, the pressure began to mount again. My heart started to pound, my pulse raced, and I was terrified. What was next? I wasn't sure I wanted to find out. The pain was the only thing that was real. The pain was something that I could understand. I couldn't control it. I couldn't harness it. But, I could understand it. Maybe there was some power in that understanding. I really wasn't sure, but I was going to be forced to find out.

Often, it's the deepest pain which empowers
you to grow into your highest self.
- Karen Salmansohn

Chapter Five: Rehab...

Nothing is more frightening than a fear you cannot name.
- Cornelia Funke

During times of intense anxiety, there was no telling how my body might react. The panic could send me reeling, or it could absolutely paralyze me. Earlier in the day, it had sent me reeling, as I flailed about on the gurney. Now, as I laid there, my arms were restrained. Even though I didn't have a choice, I figured the paralyzing fear would suit me better this time. As the ambulance doors opened, I let that fear overcome me.

Like a child, I shook. I couldn't control it. I wanted to pretend it was because of the cold, but I knew that wasn't true. I tried to lie to myself, but the churning in my stomach called me a liar. The sunlight hit my face, and I closed my eyes, hoping not to open them again. I thought about my failures, and how I didn't deserve to be alive. The gurney continued past the first set of doors. This entrance was supposed to symbolize hope and a second chance. For me, it symbolized a terrifying realization that my life was never going to be the same.

As I was forced through another set of doors, I was shook from my thoughts. I wouldn't be able to day dream through all of this. I couldn't just sleep it all away. I opened my eyes as I was pushed through a long, seemingly endless, corridor. The maze of doors and hallways was all a blur. The blandness of the walls and ceiling tired me, but my extreme nervousness wouldn't allow me to rest.

My stomach was screaming at me. The nervousness I was feeling was tearing at my insides. Fear was gripping me. Finally, after what seemed like an eternity, we came to a halt at the base of two very large steel security doors. Each door appeared thick and heavy. No handles were present, and each door contained a tiny bullet proof window with one way glass. Whatever lingered behind the door could see me, but I could not see it. The increasing uncertainty made me feel nauseous. Pains pierced my abdomen as thoughts bounced around my head.

To my right was a large counter. It too was surrounded by bullet proof glass. A small nurse sat behind the counter and smiled as the paramedics passed paperwork through a small slot at the base of the counter. Few words were spoken between them. I felt a slight sense of normalcy as I realized they had been through this drill before. I wasn't the first person to end up here. And, with the struggles of life, I, unfortunately, would not be the last.

I let that thought fester in my mind. It began to take on a life of its own. Like a rat, it scurried to each dark portion of my brain, desperately trying to hide from the light. It gnawed at me as an overwhelming sadness consumed my soul. I wasn't the only one who had come face to face with death. I wasn't the only one who had felt the hopelessness of the night. I wondered why others felt despair, how they coped with that unshakable sadness that led them here, and how they hoped to heal. The sadness of my thoughts was consuming my soul.

I wasn't sure any amount of medication, sedation, or therapy was going to help. I didn't want to share my problems with others. Hell, they were my problems. They had their own stuff to deal with. I just wanted to be alone. I wanted to sit on my bed with a pen and paper and just let the words flow. For now, I had to fake a smile and nod my head. I would just do what they asked so I could do what I really wanted to do. I really just wanted to sleep in my own bed for a very long time.

As I watched the paramedic and the nurse look over my paperwork, I decided I would become a puppet. I would participate in group sessions, and tell them what they wanted to hear. I would smile and laugh to make it appear as though I was on the mend. All I wanted to do was go home. So, whatever it took, I was going to get there.

Suddenly, my jumbled thoughts, the first cognizant ones that I had in quite some time, were interrupted by the opening of the two large doors. The loony bin was about to open up to me. I was being accepted as crazy enough to enter this place. It was not something I could grasp nor accept. How I had gotten here was known to me, but it was still a mystery. Despite all my success in school, sports, with friends, and even in work, I landed in this place. As the doors spread wide, a shiver went down my spine. While I didn't think it was possible, I was instantly more terrified than I had been the night before.

The possibilities, the opportunities, the blessings in my life; I had thrown them all away. Just as quickly as they came in, I buried them with a single unstable act. Regardless, I was terrified of what was before me. I had no idea what to expect, but none of that really mattered anymore.

As I passed through the large metal doors, they shut loudly behind me. I jumped at the sound, whipping my head around to look behind me. My body quivered, and my knees felt weak. A nurse and an armed guard walked into the passage way between the large doors I had just passed, and the ones in front of me. The nurse smiled as she slowly approached me. My mind was playing tricks on me as I shivered nervously. No matter how hard I tried, I couldn't stop shaking. While I was safe, my fight or flight response was kicking in. I couldn't control it, and I wasn't sure I would try to even if I could. Panic tied my stomach in knots, and beads of sweat began to run down my brow. I felt the color run from my face. Suddenly, I was woozy. I laid my head back down to avoid passing out.

The nurse spoke softly to me. She told me to relax. I tried to do what she said. I tried to take slow, deep, and even breaths. They helped to slow my dramatic heart rate. My legs still felt weak, but my body had stopped shaking. The nurse slowly loosened the restraints on my wrists. I was grateful to have them off. I rubbed my sweaty wrists, feeling the indentions the straps had formed on my skin. I shook my wrists in an attempt to get the blood flowing again. The nurse helped me into a sitting position. The overpowering dizziness followed. I closed my eyes, but that only made it worse. I tried to slow my breathing as I focused my eyes on the orange jumpsuit that was laid on the gurney. There was that word again... "SUICIDE".

For some reason, I couldn't shake that word. It was everywhere. It was in my file, printed on my bracelet, and now it would be printed on my clothes. I felt like Hester Prynne as I was being forced to wear my problems on my sleeve. If you are asking who Hester Prynne is, try to take yourself back to middle school. You probably met her *Scarlet Letter* there. I could feel her pain now as my issues were being broadcasted loud and clear.

As my dizziness subsided, I swung my feet off the gurney towards the floor. For a moment, I just sat on the edge of the bed. I closed my eyes, and I pictured Meagan's beautiful smile. I missed her deeply. I wondered if she knew where I was. I wondered what she would think about me now. I couldn't blame her for leaving me if that was what she ended up deciding. I wasn't sure I could be with myself, so I didn't think anyone else would want to be.

I let my rear end slide off the edge of the bed as my bare feet touched the floor for the first time. The floor was cold. My knees were stiff and weak. I shook. I wasn't sure if it was due to the fear, the hunger, or the meds. But, I shook uncontrollably, and I cried.

I closed my eyes and thought about being anywhere but here. The voice of the nurse snapped me out of it. As I slowly stripped off my blue hospital gown, the tears continued to fall. My heart was racing as I was searched up and down. Cavities and crevices were expertly searched. Uncomfortably, I pulled the orange jumpsuit on to my skinny, naked frame. It was itchy and smelt like cheap laundry detergent. Plastered on the right leg, the left chest pocket, and the back were the words "SUICIDE" in large, black, haunting font. Finally, the last shred of dignity, if I had any, was taken from me. Embarrassed and ashamed, I stood there sobbing, shaking, and covered with that horrible, demeaning label. But, I had earned it.

I approached the other set of large steel security doors. I waited as a noisy buzzer screeched, and a soft voice came over the intercom system. The doors began to open slowly. They opened just wide enough for me to enter, and I was greeted by a middle aged, clean shaven doctor sporting a salt and pepper comb over. His smile was welcoming, but somehow I knew I wasn't in Kansas anymore. Somehow, I knew that ruby red slippers wouldn't help me. The shakes were still there, but my mind was overwhelmed. Anxiety was overcoming me as I tried to hold it together.

The doctor spoke softly to me, and explained where I was, and why I was there. It irritated me that I had to rehash the same event over and over again. I wanted to shout at the top of my lungs. My emotions were devastating me. I struggled to hold them in. I bit my tongue until the pain was too much. It bled as my eyes continued to drop tears.

I was led to a large dayroom filled with chairs and an eclectic group of people. Like fresh meat, I entered the room scared and shaking. I just stared at the ground. The carpet was old and dirty. Stains littered the floor. The tables and chairs were bolted to the wall. The walls were bland and boring. But, if those walls could talk, like my moon, they would have some horrific stories of sorrow and despair to share.

Motivational posters of kittens hanging from tree limbs and an eagle snatching a fish were taped to the door. The door had been kicked, punched, head butted, and scratched. It was a beaten piece of wood, but it still stood there.

I hobbled to the nearest seat, never looking up. My eyes were transfixed on the horrible carpet. I couldn't help but think about how the stained carpet represented me. It was worn out, forever stained, and in need of desperate repair. I sat quietly, still looking downwards, and held back whatever tears I could. I choked back sobs, but I am sure they were noticeable.

Suddenly, my head jerked up wildly as I felt a hand grasp my shoulder. I nearly jumped out of my seat. The eerie combination of anxiety, fear, and overwhelming sorrow mixed with a regime of pills put me on a serious edge. The hand patted my shoulder softly, and a voice whispered to me. It was a young lady, probably a year or two older than me. Her eyes were bloodshot and swollen, probably from a mishmash of crying, lack of sleep, and medication. Her eyes were soft but dark. There was a great deal of pain hiding in those eyes. She tried to hide it behind a beautiful smile and a friendly demeanor. At least, that was my theory. The theory wasn't new to me. I had used it myself on a number of occasions. I would share a smile, a laugh, and act upbeat in order to keep my deep, dark secrets hidden.

As my eyes locked with hers, her smile widened, and she brought up her left hand to brush her long black hair behind her ear. As she did, her sleeve slipped down to her forearm, revealing a number of deep, painful looking scars. Her carved wrist was red. Puffy scars traveled a considerable length from her palms to the middle of her forearm. My bloodshot eyes gazed at the horrific image as it locked them in a trance. Slowly, I closed my eyes as tears began to fill them. I held them closed for what seemed like an eternity. I hoped that she didn't catch the surprise and pain on my face as I stared at the painful reminders of her moments of utter despair.

I felt the terrible pain radiating from her scarred and battered body. In that singular moment, my mind was consumed with the unimaginable hurt that must have engulfed her poor, sweet, tattered heart. As I sat there, with my eyes still closed, I was removed from my current predicament. For a short time, I was no longer overcome with my own emotions. The pain that consumed my senses melted away as I realized that I wasn't the only one under such distress.

As my eyes opened, allowing tears to escape, they were greeted by the same smile they closed on. I cracked a small smile back as she introduced herself. With that, the young lady held out her hand, her sleeve once again falling down and exposing the struggles of her life. We shared a playful high-five, which brought a smile to my face. In an instant, she bounded off.

I sat pondering this random encounter. Considering the situation we were all in, it took a great deal of courage for her to come over to me, share a smile, a high-five, and introduce herself. The moment that she made me forget about my pain, no matter how brief it was, was truly remarkable.

Those carefree, almost happy, feelings were short lived however. As I continued to sit nervously, staring downward at the stained carpet, the tears returned. They streamed, slowly at first, from the corners of my bloodshot eyes. I shook. My heart raced as I pondered how I had ended up here. "Here" was a relative term. I didn't ponder how I ended up sitting in my current predicament. No, I didn't ponder how I ended up sitting in a mental hospital, institutionalized, as some put it. My mind pondered the subtle twists and turns of my life that led me to doing things that landed me here. That was the "here" I contemplated.

I thought about the disease that imprisoned my heart. Depression was without prejudice. It infected whomever possible, by wrapping its horrific tentacles and tightening its terrible grasp. It strived to infect as many people as possible regardless of gender, race, creed, or age. It attacked the rich and the poor, the loved and the lonely. It battled those in relationships, and those without. It fought with success and failure. It pushed for retribution. Depression was deceptive and held in captivity those desperate feelings of self-worth and love. It was slowly killing me, as well as, the group of people here.

"Who's your buddy...who's your friend?!!" A raspy voice sent shivers down my spine as my thoughts were interrupted. An uncomfortable energy overcame me as a horribly pockmarked face came within inches of mine. For a brief moment, the intruding nose came in contact with mine. The greasy beard smiled widely displaying the few blackened teeth left. Giggles escaped his mouth. The smell of his breath attacked my nose as I held back the gags. He smiled widely, turned his head sideways like a dog and shouted, "Who's your buddy...who's your friend?!!" When I didn't say anything back, his smile disappeared, and a scowl consumed his face.

His voice rose. He stood on the chair next to me, and he lifted his hands upwards towards the heavens. He kept his dark eyes pointed downwards to Hell. His powerful voice bellowed "Satan, my Lord, speak to me. Beelzebub, Belial, Lucifer!" His bellows continued, "And there appeared another wonder in heaven; and behold a great red dragon, having seven heads and ten horns, and seven crowns upon his head. And his tail drew the third part of the stars of heaven, and did cast them to earth: and the dragon stood before the woman which was ready to be delivered, for to devour her child as soon as it was born (Revelations 12:3-4)."

"Satan, I am of the third. Tell me thy will."

"And the GREAT DRAGON was thrown down, the ancient serpent, who is called the devil and Satan, the deceiver of the whole world – he was thrown down to the earth, and his angels were thrown down with him (Revelations 12:9)."

"I am with thee, yea even a Prince of Darkness."

His voice trailed off. He pointed at me, and he laughed in the most menacing manner. Seeing my discomfort, he continued,

"Behold, I will corrupt your seed, and spread dung upon your faces, even the dung of your solemn feasts; and one shall take you away with it (Malachi 2:3)."

His eyes were dark and cold as he stared into mine. As I began to look away, a smile formed on his face. He giggled wildly, ran his hands through his greasy hair, and said "Who's your buddy...who's your friend?" Giggling, he jumped off the chair and shuffled away.

If I wasn't uncomfortable before, I definitely was now. Over the next 24 hours, scenes like the one above happened regularly. Multiple patients had to be sedated in the middle of group sessions. Horrible screams, heart-breaking cries, and horrific moans could be heard from down the hall as patients were dragged away. I sat, still in my chair, looking down at the carpet. Stained and dirty, like me, we understood one another.

During group, I would put a smile on face, and I'd tell the doctors exactly what I thought they wanted to hear. They were thrilled with my positive outlook on treatment and life. My renewed zest for happiness surprised them, and they looked to build upon it. By the end of the first six hours, the doctor was ready to allow me to move out of maximum security. I would be off of constant suicide watch. He wouldn't sign off on it though, not until I made it through the night.

Night. I hadn't feared the night for quite some time. When I was 7, I was terrified of being in our basement at night. My room was in the basement, across the hall from my older brother's room. As the ghosts ran rampant down there, he would sleep with no problem. Somehow, he didn't see the ghosts that inhabited that place, but I sure did. I was terrified. In a desperate effort to help me overcome my fears, my parents bought me a Ghostbusters Proton pack. Dr. Egon Spengler's design hit the spot. I would be down in the basement at 2 in the morning using my particle accelerator to charge my particle beam in order to weaken the ghosts, and eventually, place them above my trap for capture. If you haven't done it, you haven't lived.

I hadn't been scared of the night for a very long time. But, on this night, I was terrified again. I secretly longed for my Proton pack. As I was shown to my room, the unfamiliarity of this entire situation put me on edge. There were no doors. Outside of each room sat a chair. A staff member sat by your room all night, watching you sleep, and ensuring you couldn't hurt yourself. The small room was consumed by the two twin beds that resided in it. Neither of them had sheets or pillows. The bathroom couldn't be used without supervision either.

Frustrated, I just laid on my mattress, curdled into a ball and tried to sleep. My roommate sobbed uncontrollably. He hadn't talked during group. He hadn't interacted during free time. He hadn't talked as I introduced myself to go to our room. He was on suicide watch, and he wore his depression on his sleeve. As he sobbed; the gravity of my situation, the events of the day, and my already fragile state hit me all at once. I began to cry, but I kept the urge to sob under control. Tears streamed down my face as I slowly fell asleep.

For the majority of the night, I tossed and turned on my thin, twin mattress. The night got cold as I shivered in my itchy jumpsuit. For a little while, I thought about all the people who had worn this same jumpsuit before me. I thought about all the people who had slept on this mattress, without any blankets to keep them warm. I thought about those who cried tears, sobbing uncontrollably just a few feet away from someone else also in pain. It brought me some perspective. Little did I know, that perspective would grow in the coming days.

The morning came far too soon. The winks of sleep were few. I felt sad for my roommate as it seemed that he cried most the night. Breakfast was delivered to our room. Everything was eaten with our hands. Silverware, even plastic ware, was forbidden. Over breakfast, I asked my roommate how he was doing, but he just glared at me. I guess it was a stupid question, but I was just trying to show concern. I continued my breakfast until the doctor called for me. Two orderlies, clad in white, came to my room, and I was escorted to the doctor's office. His comb over was looking as stellar as ever today, and I made sure to let him know that.

After a timely discussion of glitter, rainbows, and unicorns, I was asked by the doctor if I was ready to move to in-house rehab treatment. I contemplated his request. While I knew that I probably wasn't ready, there was no way that I was going to spend another night on suicide watch. I couldn't handle the sobs of my roommate, the sermons from the Prince of Darkness, and the itchiness of the orange jumpsuit. It was time to go. It was time to make an effort to recover.

All great changes are preceded by chaos.
- Deepak Chopra

Chapter Six: The Lucky Penny...

Your task is not to seek for love, but merely to seek and find all the barriers within yourself that you have built against it.
- Rumi

The past 24 hours had been a whirlwind of chaos that turned me into a nervous wreck, someone beyond recognition. Although the salt and pepper comb over had agreed to move me off suicide watch, and into in-house rehab treatment, I was on edge. My orange jumpsuit had been replaced by a pair of cotton shorts and a white t-shirt. While the suicide label had been removed from my clothes, it still resided on my bracelet, as well as my broken heart.

Freedom, to some extent, was coming my way. It scared me. It was a bizarre sensation to be terrified of it. I was fearful of things that seemed so common. Actions that I had done a million times made me apprehensive. The idea of sleeping, without supervision, caused me some serious anxiety. The thought of making my own decisions was grounds for a crushing uneasiness to overcome me. At some point, I was going to have to face these common freedoms. Hopefully, I could overcome the fear.

As I sat in the common area, I pondered my very existence. For some reason, I was still here. It had been a rollercoaster, a ride that I was not prepared for, nor was it a ride I desired. But, I had purchased a ticket, stood patiently in line, pulled down my lap bar, and put my hands in the air. Maybe, putting my hands in the air was truly a signal of surrender, but somehow I still ended up on this wild, unpredictable ride.

My new found freedoms were not bestowed upon me immediately. They had to be earned. Progress would grant me levels and privileges. As I progressed, I would be able to do more things on my own. I would be allowed to go to the dining hall, walk the grounds, and get more visits from family and friends. For now, I sat around in the dayroom playing Solitaire, waiting to see my parents for the first time since the hospital.

As I thought of them coming to see me, it upset my stomach. My feelings were mixed. The chaotic jumble of emotions that skipped around my heart and head confused me. I was happy that they were coming to see me, but I wasn't ready to face everyone. I wasn't ready for the tears. I wasn't prepared for the questions. It was inevitable. They would come eventually. The how and the why would be thrown my way. I was not ready to answer any of those questions.

In reality, I still didn't have a clue. I had no idea why I did what I did. I was still trying to figure out all the answers on my own. I was a tangled web of lies, sorrow, and unresolved issues; all of which had to be sorted through, in my time. At some point, I would have to face the firing squad, whether I was ready to or not.

I did have some ideas about why certain things happened, but the answers would not suffice those who didn't understand. If someone had never visited the ultimate pits of despair and been trapped in the clutches of depression, then they would not understand the how or why. They couldn't understand, nor did I think they would. It wasn't that I thought they should understand, but I hoped, in time, they would try.

As my parents came in for their first visit, I was nervous. But, it went surprising well. As much as they probably wanted to, my parents refrained from asking why. Actually, we kept the conversation casual. We talked about the food and the weather. My dad and I talked about sports and running. My mom asked if

I needed anything, and she told me that she loved me. It was all very casual, far too casual for my current surroundings. Most of the time, someone was leaving this place in tears. For us, we had mostly laughs and smiles.

As I was still getting acclimated to my new surroundings, I decided not to go into detail about the night before. I didn't share the sermons from the Prince of Darkness, the discussions I had with the comb over, or the night of tears. After all, I didn't want to worry my mom.

I had been terrified, and I had shed my share of tears the night before. A great deal of stress was lifted off my shoulders when I lost the orange jumpsuit. I had survived the scary side of the loony bin. At least one fear had been lifted. With my clothes no longer plastered with that demeaning word, I felt like I was making progress. It was ironic to me, almost funny, that our entire youth years are consumed by labels on clothes, but in that moment, I was never so happy for a cheap, plain Wal-Mart t-shirt and pair of shorts.

When my parents left, it was bittersweet. I knew that they were extremely disappointed, but I knew they loved me unconditionally, and their concern was deeply overwhelming. I knew that I could count on them just like I did before this incident. The love was there, and the healing was ready to begin. I knew it would be a long, slow process, but I never realized how long it would truly take.

In my new environment, group sessions were a little less intimidating. Everyone faked being supportive, and no one asked to be my buddy or friend after speaking to the devil. The absence of that is something that always makes someone feel a little more comfortable with their surroundings. I was surrounded by other patients suffering from depression. There were also patients suffering from drug and/or alcohol addiction. The variety of people was supposed to make everyone more concerned with learning from others. Some of us knew how we had ended up here, while others still had no idea.

My roommate was coming down off heroin. He had been a heroin addict in Salt Lake City for a year. He almost overdosed while shooting up outside of a McDonald's after his girlfriend dumped him. The police found him strung out, his veins collapsed, and naked in his Toyota Celica.

His name was Luis. He was a legal immigrant from Mexico. He had worked every job you could imagine. In California, while working in the fruit fields, he got introduced to heroin. He had followed the trail to Salt Lake City, where he could shoot up with a better product for a cheaper price. He was just 25 years old, and his dad had made a small fortune playing Powerball scratch tickets. When he was arrested, his dad sent him here. It was far better than the alternative, because Luis almost ended up in prison.

Luis was an addict, completely dependent on the drug. At night, he would cry. He would turn pale, as his eyes would glaze over. He would fidget uncontrollably as the urge to use would overcome him. He would slap his arm, working his veins, what was left of them, into a wild frenzy. He would sweat profusely until he was drenched. He would toss and turn on his bed, letting out whines of discomfort. He would vomit, often and in large quantities. His body yearned for a needle. His tracks were dark and painful looking. His arms were bruised, up and down, on both sides. I would help him to the bathroom over and over again. Sometimes, he would just have me help him sit in the shower, and then, turn on the cold water, full blast. He would just sit there, in his clothes, sobbing.

His English was broken, but we could communicate. We used hand motions and laughed a lot when we tried to get our points across. He would apologize every morning, and thank me for my assistance. It was no big deal. It actually helped me more than it helped him. I needed the distraction. I needed the perspective. There it is. I told you that it would be back. Perspective. Luis was helping me get one. I was appreciative of it.

The next day, I stood in the rec room, listening to a former meth head play guitar and sing Bob Marley's "Redemption Song". His acoustic melody was brilliant. His smooth voice conveyed a message of hope. In my head, I wondered if his talent would be lost to drugs. If he had been selling a CD, I would have bought it in an instant. He sang "Buffalo Soldier" and "Three Little Birds". As I listened to him, I felt some peace.

In an instant, I turned into a nervous wreck. I paced back and forth, sighed, and felt dizzy. As I stared in disbelief at the nurse's station, I started to cry. There, standing next to my parents, was Meagan. I rubbed my eyes in disbelief. I smiled widely, but I was incredibly nervous. Eight months into our delicate relationship, she was suddenly confronted by the fact that her boyfriend suffered from serious depression, had a suicide attempt, and was currently residing in a nut house.

We had been trying the long distance relationship for a couple months now. I was quickly becoming a prime option to bring home to visit her mom and dad. Maybe they would let me wear my jumpsuit to drive home my increasing value. As she approached me, she smiled. Still, I wasn't sure if I was getting a hug or a slap. Her warm embrace was comforting, but I wasn't sure just how much she knew.

As we talked, through tears, I explained what I had done. I told her that I understood if she wanted to end things, because I was a mess. Instead, she took my hand and squeezed it tight. She reached into her jean pocket and pulled out a penny.

It was tarnished. It was dirty. It was beaten and battered. Much like the condition of my heart at that time, it had been brighter, shinier, and seen better days. Still, it was a beautiful penny. It would become a vessel for memories, hopes, and dreams. That soiled penny had traveled limitless miles, and it exchanged countless hands before it ended up in mine. As it passed from her soft, gentle hands to mine, I smiled.

Eighteen years ago, when that little penny was pressed with Lincoln's head, I would have never imagined it would become so important to me. That flawed, imperfect piece of copper from 1987, which must have been a pretty stellar year, found its way to my heart. It symbolized love, and an attempt to understand my troubled soul. It would become a symbol of what it meant to be alive.

Love me when I least deserve it, because
that's when I really need it.
- Swedish Proverb

Chapter Seven: Topher...

*Great perils have this beauty, that they
bring to light the fraternity of strangers.
- Victor Hugo*

After a nerve-racking twenty four hours on suicide watch, a move to in-house rehab, and a couple visits, I was beginning to settle in. This area of the hospital allowed patients much more freedom. It was quite the change. Sheets covered the beds, bathrooms and showers could be used without supervision, and you were able to have some of your belongings in your room. The freedom, while still scary, was a welcomed change.

For me, my new found freedoms were almost as terrifying as my time on suicide watch. While that might seem ironic, it was true. I was more scared of the thought of freedom than anything. Freedom made me wonder if I would hurt myself again. Freedom granted me the ability to make more mistakes, to cause more hurt, and to be alone. So, for the first time in my life, I was afraid of freedom. I was terrified to be able to do whatever I wanted to do.

Intimidated, I entered the next chapter of rehab. "Level 3: Embracing Freedom" was a big step in recovery. I should have been excited, but I wasn't. I was surprised and a little disappointed. I had used lies to make my way through the first 36 hours in an attempt to get out of this place. I had acted upbeat and chipper. I had told my therapist what she wanted to hear. I had twisted words, faked feelings, and hid tears. It was all in an attempt to escape the true pain and desperation I had been feeling. Maybe the lies were the best thing for me.

The Scrabble tiles sat neatly displayed on the wooden tray in front of me. My fingers fiddled with a blank tile, feeling its smoothness. It danced in my hand as it rolled over my fingers and dropped to the table. The noise broke the silence, echoing throughout the deserted hallway. I smiled, quietly picked up the tile, and placed it beside the rest of my collection. Each little wooden piece represented an opportunity. If placed in the proper location, each of the tiles could dramatically change the game. Even the most subtle of moves could alter the outcome. Scrabble had become a release, a time of positivity. A game that I rarely played before had become a form of therapy. Scrabble was bringing perspective. Scrabble was bringing understanding. Scrabble with Topher was bringing forgiveness and healing while teaching me about life.

Topher and I were an unlikely pair to say the least. Like most unlikely pairs, for some reason, we worked. We only shared three things in common; we loved to write, we were broken, and we were in denial. There may have been more things that brought us to the common ground that we currently stood on, but those didn't really seem relevant. We were both in desperate need of some serious medical help.

We loved words, and while neither of us wanted to verbally express them...we both loved putting them on paper. So, in a short time, Scrabble became a logical, even desirable, outlet for us. When a lined piece of paper would no longer suffice, when a pen in hand was no longer adequate; the Scrabble board was placed on a card table in the hallway, and the games began.

We would sit for hours, often getting interrupted by therapists, nurses, group sessions, and medicine roll call. More often than not, we would ditch group as we felt our Scrabble sessions were more important, more influential, and absolutely necessary in our healing processes. I am not sure if that was actually true, but we told ourselves that. Group was supposed to be a touchy feely coming together of strangers. Each person sharing his or her problems as others listened intently. The discussing of issues and resolutions, the setting of goals, and the obligatory pats on the back would follow. It all seemed so fake, so insincere. So, on most occasions, we would not attend. More often than not, we would be caught ditching. In those instances, our Scrabble game would be interrupted, our journals would be closed, and we would be urged incessantly to go to group. To those requests, we would agree out of necessity rather than actual desire. After all, it was required treatment according to our shrinks.

Our normal lack of attendance wasn't because we felt superior to the wonderful group process. It was more that the process just didn't fit us. Our solitary writing sessions, and our "group" sessions through discussion and Scrabble were far more therapeutic. The feelings of inadequacy, the worries of judgment, and the setting of pressure disappeared when it was just us. We could talk for hours. We shared stories. We read each other's written words. For some reason, the treatment plan we prescribed was welcomed, and it seemed far more effective.

It all started on my first evening off of suicide watch. I sat in the rec room, my head in my hands, attempting to hold back the tears. A gentleman with long brown hair, and a well-kept goatee, leaned back in the chair across from me with a notebook in hand. He had been scribbling notes from time to time. He looked like a Venice Beach hippy with hemp bracelets covering his wrists and numerous rings on his fingers. As I sat there, I could feel his eyes on me. When I looked up, he stood up and walked over to me. He patted me on the shoulder as he introduced himself. Over a game of Yahtzee, we talked. It felt good to speak to someone who didn't know me. There was no judgment.

When medicine call came, I took a fairly high dose of Serquel for the first time. The doctor was playing with my medications, and the dosage was higher than expected. As our Yahtzee game continued, I began to get loopy. The room was spinning. I couldn't keep my balance. I fell out of my chair, and I laughed until I cried. Topher had seen it before, and he kindly escorted me to my room, sat me on my bed, and left. That night, I slept for the first time in a really long time.

Topher and I were strangely different, and yet, we were eerily similar. He was almost a decade older than me. As his twenties were ending, mine were just beginning. Our experiences were vastly different. We lived in different places, and we believed in different things. Despite those differences, we understood one another. That wonderful understanding couldn't have come at a better time.

As I had entered rehab, I didn't believe that there was another human being walking upon God's green Earth that could understand me. In the moments since I had entered this place, I didn't think that there was anyone who would look at me without judgmental eyes. I had wondered if there was a single person that wouldn't ask me why. So, when I met Topher, and there were no prerequisites to his genuine concern, I was amazed. I felt a deep sense of gratitude for the friendship he extended. It extended past the barriers I had constructed. Topher, like me, was hurting. He was broken too, which enabled him to look beyond my shortcomings. The fragility of our situations strengthened our bond. While our situations were very different, we came together in an attempt to heal.

Topher was a writer. He had published numerous short stories and a science fiction novel. All of which, he had written while he was under the influence of extensive amounts of alcohol and prescription drugs. His growing abuse of substances had led to him overdosing in his office while attempting to finish his latest masterpiece. The overdose would have taken his life, but his best friend just happened to stop by to check on him. He found him, choking on his own vomit, unable to help himself. Without the divine intervention of a concerned friend, Topher wouldn't have been around. Topher would have died, alone in his office. His latest manuscript of his struggles would have never been finished. Instead, he sat across the Scrabble board, changing his view from the tiles that sat strewn along his tray and the manuscript of some 400-odd pages that he had written. His red pen moved haphazardly over the pages, scratching changes to his words of meaning. Occasionally, as he read, a tear would escape his eye. I found solace in those rare, authentic moments.

Topher encouraged me to write. He read my journal, and he helped push me to share the feelings that I kept hidden in the dark corners of my soul. In reality, the words written here are an acknowledgment of Topher and his unrelenting pursuit to help me find some sort of solace in my life. After Scrabble, I would dig into his manuscript as he reviewed my journal. His red pen would share notes of constructive criticism, ideas for the future, and words of steady encouragement. I would juggle a blue pen in my hand as it danced around on his manuscript. As I read his tragic story of loss and sadness, perspective was before me. My tears became his tears, and his became mine. We were united in the unique and eye opening perspectives of one another.

When Scrabble or writing wasn't enough, we would sit in the dayroom trying to get each other to laugh at the most ridiculous things. We would practice standup comedy routines that were notoriously bad. We would laugh at bad jokes and poor innuendo. Still, the laughs, no matter the content, were welcomed.

During the group sessions, the ones that we were forced to attend, we were no longer allowed to sit next to each other. We caused too much of a disturbance. So, like elementary school children, we were separated. That didn't stop us though. We would sit across from each other, and attempt to make each other laugh out loud. When one of us achieved success, one, or both of us, would be removed, which was what we wanted.

In a group session for art therapy, we were coloring skeletons in top hats. I am not really sure why, but it was supposed to be therapeutic. Needless to say, Topher and I thought it was a tragic waste of time. Topher kept holding up his picture to show to me. I wasn't sure why. He had colored it nicely, and he placed a decent amount of glitter in the skeleton's genital region. I chuckled at this, but it was not his best work. Without warning, he jammed his index finger through the paper where the glitter was. The skeleton was now of the male variety. In his other hand, he held up a sign "What happens in Vegas...lands you in rehab".

It was corny. It was juvenile. It made me laugh until I was kicked out of group. As I walked sheepishly out of the session, Topher followed with a big grin on his face. He had won, and it was time for Scrabble.

A man that was a complete stranger just days earlier became the one person who I found the most solace in. He was the one who encouraged me. We learned from one another. In those moments, Topher truly changed my life in ways that I never would have thought possible. I was indebted to him, and hopefully, in at least some small way, he was indebted to me.

On very rare occasion, the pathway is smoothed
by the least expected. One of our fellow weary
travelers helps us brave the desolate road ahead.
In those times, the blessings of a stranger helps the
healing process begin before we realize that it even started.
- Unknown

Chapter Eight: Freedom…

Mistakes are the portals of discovery.
- James Joyce

I awoke, drenched in a cold sweat. Beads of perspiration dripped from my forehead. My sheets were completely soaked. Slowly, I ran a shaky hand over my head. The side effects of my medications were quickly starting to show. A terrifying nightmare had awoken me. It left my heart pounding. I held back the tears as I looked over at the empty bed next to mine. I was alone.

Luis had punched his ticket out of rehab the night before. His dad, once again, had come to the rescue. He was being transferred to a drug rehab center in Los Angeles, which left me alone in room #7. I hated being alone. I hated the quiet. Luckily though, my nightly medication knocked me out immediately. With the deep sleep came the side effects. Nightmares, night sweats, the shakes, and the suicidal ideation would come for me. It couldn't be controlled.

I crawled out of my bed, disgusted with the sweat that covered my body. I desperately wished to stop taking the medications, but I couldn't. I needed them. Without them, I would never sleep. Without them, I was scared of myself. In reality, I was always scared of myself. The medication numbed me, making that fear a little easier to control.

As I stripped off my clothes, I stared at the mirror in front of me. I was terrified of the image that stared back. I had lost too much weight. My skin stretched tightly over my bones. I was so pale. My eyes were puffy, red, and surrounded by a deep blackness. It wasn't me. It couldn't have been.

Today was supposed to by my final day in rehab. I wasn't ready to leave, but I didn't want to stay. The fear of myself had gotten worse since I started the regimen of anti-depressants. I didn't want to admit that however. In doing so, it would require the doctors to experiment with new medications, and I wasn't ready for that. The growing list of side-effects wasn't worth the "supposed" cure.

I quickly got dressed and left my room. I wandered down the hallway to room #2. I expected to find Topher in his final preparations. He was being transferred to a new facility, which really left me with no reason to stay. As I entered the room, it was empty. He had left early, while I was still enduring my latest night terror. On his nightstand, there stood an envelope. In flowing script, my name adorned it. On the corner, as a joke, there was a small amount of glitter. Next to it, he had written, "What happens in Vegas, makes you successful."

With tears in my eyes, I nervously picked up the envelope and left the room. For the first time since I met Topher, I walked to breakfast, alone. As I sat, playing with my scrambled eggs, I stared at the envelope. I couldn't bring myself to open it. I just sat there, squishing my eggs with my spork, as I thought about what I had learned from him. In time, I would read his words. For now, I decided to let them remain a mystery.

As the day progressed, I found myself playing Scrabble. Alone, I sat at the table in the hallway, playing tiles off both sides of the table. When it was time for group, I slowly walked to the conference room. Quietly, I participated for the entire session. I didn't laugh. I didn't get separated. I didn't get asked to leave. I didn't care.

My parents and Meagan arrived shortly before lunch. We shared a meal in the dining hall, the last of my time there. As we spent the reminder of the afternoon meeting with therapists, doctors, and administrators, I grew very tired. I was ready for this all to end. As I packed up the few items in my room, I caught myself staring at the envelope. I sat on the edge of my bed, holding it in my hands, unsure of what to do. Tears started to stream down my face. I slowly opened the most important piece of mail that I would ever receive.

The letter, seven pages in all, contained the most beautifully written words that I have ever read. My heart was immediately filled with gratitude. I was overcome with love. In that moment, I thanked God endlessly for Topher's timely intervention. His attempt to understand me was only the beginning. His letter wasn't the end, and I planned to see him again.

I carefully slid the cherished letter into my bag, picked up my journal, and left room #7 for the final time. In the top drawer of the nightstand, I left a letter of my own; leaving with it, the yearning that someone, anyone, would find solace in my meager words. I would never know if anyone did, but, in room #7, I left my blood, sweat, and tears.

As I made my final walk down the hallway, tears trickled down my face as I smiled.

The ride home was quiet. It was a weird feeling to have the freedom to leave the facility. I felt like an escapee, on the run, and nervous. The entire experience had been surreal. The journey wasn't one that I was ready to accept, but it was one that I had to continue.

When I arrived home, I just stared at the front door. I wasn't ready to enter the place where I had almost ended my life. I couldn't look at the kitchen, the hallway, or my bedroom. I couldn't handle the slow motion replay of my mistakes. Still, in order to recover, I knew I had to face it. I had to face my demons, and it was going to have to start with a trip to that cupboard.

I entered the house, apprehensively, at first. Flashbacks of that night flooded my mind. I saw myself gagging down pills, collapsing in the hallway, and crawling to my room. I shook as my knees weakened. I had to sit down. I cried.

I faced my brother and sister, both were supportive, but neither could understand. They hugged me, told me that they loved me, and reminded me that I could confide in them. As time slowly ticked away, I realized Meagan wouldn't be able to stay forever. Soon, she would have to leave. I would have to confide in someone; my brother, my sister, my dad, my mom, someone.

Over the next few days, Meagan kept me company. I smiled countless times over those days. Life seemed to be getting better. We played games, we kissed, and we snuggled until she fell asleep. Maybe I would be alright. Maybe everything would be okay. If we could stay like this forever, maybe I would survive.

While I hated the side effects of my medications, I was doing better on them. I slept some at night, but I was always awoken by nightmares about self-harm and suicide. I would be covered in sweat, shaking, and scared. For those nights, Meagan was right there. She was there to comfort me. She was there to hold me. She was there to love me.

Meagan had immediately boarded a flight after my sister had called her. When she received the news that I was in the hospital, she didn't hesitate. She didn't question why. She didn't ask how. She just purchased a plane ticket and flew to Salt Lake. She had skipped school, left family, and rearranged her life for me. As soon as she could be by my side, she was. The moment she gave me the Lucky Penny, I knew she was my soul mate. I loved her more deeply and passionately than I could have ever imagined.

Before I knew it though, it was time for her to leave. That kiss, the one in the airport before she left, crushed me as it completed me. I hated watching her go, but I knew it was only a matter of time before I saw her again.

I laid in bed that night, missing Meagan, and feeling scared. I tossed and turned as I thought about the cupboard. I needed to face it. I had to see it. My body was pulled to it. I slowly crawled out of bed and walked to the kitchen. There I stood, in front of it, staring. I touched my forehead, feeling the knot from that night. I started to breakdown as I remembered myself falling to the ground, my head hitting the countertop on the way. My heart raced, pounding uncontrollably. With a trembling hand, I reached for the cupboard door, and I sobbed. I had to face the demons that resided inside. That cupboard represented the depths of my soul. Inside, I would find the pain, the regret, and the hate.

I stared in disbelief. The cupboard was empty. The bottles of medications were no longer there. Instead, they had been replaced by an unconditional love. Inside, all that remained was a beautiful card from my mom and dad. The card expressed unwavering hope, deep understanding, and a never ending love. The words scribbled inside were soothing to read. As I read them, tears streamed down my face. I had faced the cupboard, and I had found love. I didn't deserve it, but it was there.

In the following days, I had my share of ups and downs. I was still adjusting to life on medication. I was still adjusting to freedom. I was still adjusting to the realizations of what I could do to myself. All of it was new, and most of it was uncomfortable.

Boulder City was my home. I missed it. I couldn't adjust to life away from Meagan. I refused to. It was becoming increasingly more difficult to be 500 miles away from her. While my family was wonderful, supportive, and loving, I had nothing else keeping me in Utah. I didn't have a job, schoolwork, or friends to keep me busy. I missed basketball on Saturday mornings. I missed working with my friends. Most of all, I missed Meagan.

I spent my long, lonely days staying as busy as possible. Besides various appointments with my therapist and psychiatrist, I had too much free time on my hands. The free time always allowed me to think. Thinking about my life was a constant struggle. In order to harness the pain, I would spill out my feelings in my journal. My thoughts of rehab, recovery, and redemption filled the pages. I would write letters to Topher, expressing my concerns, answering his inquiries, and sharing passages from my journal. Still, I wondered if my life would become anything more than it currently was.

I feared the night. I hid my thoughts of suicide, desperately wishing that without acknowledgement, they would disappear. I slowly began to confide in my sister. We would cruise to the nearest fast food joints, ordering "cat food tacos" and "fat girl food". On those late night drives, we would talk. I kept many of my dark secrets hidden from her, but her company always helped.

She would quietly listen to me for as long as we drove. If I didn't feel like talking, we would jam to the radio. We would rap Eminem songs, sing Backstreet Boys, and rock out to Aerosmith. She was becoming another light in my life, quietly helping me through my struggles.

Despite her help, I knew I needed a change. I need to be back at work, back in school, and back with Meagan. I planned to move back to Boulder City. I struggled with leaving my family. Their support was incredibly heartwarming, but I needed something more. I wasn't sure what it was, but I needed to leave to find out.

Eventually, I convinced my parents that moving back to Boulder City was the best thing for me. When I finally decided to move, I didn't tell Meagan that I was coming home. Instead, I called her to let her know that it would be a couple of weeks before I could see her. She was disappointed, but she understood. After we ended our conversation, I hugged my parents, got into my car, and headed down I-15 towards home.

I was nervous of the freedom the open road provided. I could go anywhere and do anything I wanted. Luckily, there was only one place I wanted to be. As I drove, I excitedly thought about things getting better. I would be able to work again, play basketball with friends, and spend time with Meagan. If that combination of things wouldn't help in the healing process, then I wasn't sure if anything else would.

That night, I pulled into her driveway. I sat in the car, genuinely excited for the first time in quite a while. I pulled a dozen roses from the passenger seat, walked to the door, and knocked. My heart pounded, and I had butterflies in my stomach. When she answered the door, I was overwhelmed by her beauty. She giggled as she kissed me. Tears filled her eyes. We stood there, on the doorstep, in a tight embrace. As we held one another, time stood still. For a moment, I felt complete. I wasn't sure how long it would last, but I didn't want to let it go. Maybe, if freedom was always like this, then I was going to be alright.

Those who love you are not fooled by mistakes you have made or dark images you hold about yourself. They remember your beauty when you feel ugly; your wholeness when you are broken; your innocence when you feel guilty; and your purpose when you are confused.
- Alan Cohen

Chapter Nine: Realizations...

I was so scared to give up depression, fearing that somehow the worst part of me was actually all of me.
- Elizabeth Wurtzel

The flickers of light from the television set flashed across my tired face. My eyes were heavy, distraught, and full of fear. A Taco Bell commercial revealed tears. A commercial for the new Chevy Silverado revealed pain. A preview for the latest blockbuster revealed horror. Empty bottles sat on the bed in front of me. The bottles were eerily similar to the ones that almost took my life a couple of months earlier. I had been released from rehab. I had left Topher. I had accepted freedom, and a bag full of pills to help me become a better person. Somehow, I was the only one to see the major holes in their master plan of recovery.

I began to tremble uncontrollably. There were pills everywhere. The horrific sight made me sob like a hungry infant. I screamed until my lungs burned. I slammed my hand down viciously on my night stand. A piercing pain quickly shot through it. It instantly began to swell. I looked upwards towards the heavens, and I begged for comfort. I appealed endless for help. I cried. I pleaded. Nothing happened. My tears continued to flow, and the uncomfortable sounds of a young man sobbing grew louder. I buried my head in my hands and violently wept.

The bottles that were once filled to the brim were now strewn chaotically across my comforter. Three-month supplies of both Luvox and Seroquel, along with handfuls of Lortab and Tylenol PM, were spread before me. I grimaced as a bright light shined across my tear stained face. My heavy eyes burned, causing me to blink wildly. I shook my head cruelly, and I slapped my face with a considerable force. My eyes widened, and I caught a glimpse of my notepad. From a distance, I read the chicken scratch of notes, sayings, quotes, and the past week's thoughts. It was a chaotic mess of a flustered mind. As the dialogue of Sportscenter began to drown my cries, a particular line of scribbled letters stuck out to me. It read, "Dad called. He said, 'hang in there, I am proud of you, and I love you."

I stared at the words. I tried to push them away. Those words didn't fit me. Not me. Proud?! Of what?! Of me?! Right! What was there to be proud of? I screamed, "What are you proud of me for? Not dying? Not being able to kill myself? Huh? What is there to be proud of?"

I swiped my hand aggressively across my bed, and it sent a cocktail of pills flying. They bounced off the wall and littered onto the floor. I punched the mattress furiously. The coils compressed with the force. The anger inside my body was overwhelming. I ran to the bathroom and began pushing my fingers down my throat. I gagged intensely and felt my diaphragm jolt. Saliva ran down my hand, and my eyes watered. I heaved again, but I couldn't make myself vomit.

I was weak. I was mentally, physically, and emotionally exhausted. The sweat on my forehead slowly trickled down to the end of my nose. As I watched it drip to the tile floor, I considered how I was back in this predicament. I was broken, and history was repeating its sad story. My state of affairs hadn't improved. Recovery hadn't really begun.

Recovery required strength. It required desire. It required a distraction, or a passion, or something tangible. I was lacking all of those things. As much as I wanted recovery to happen, it was not something that was going to happen overnight. It was going to be a continual process of acceptance, understanding, effort, and love. For those who have suffered from depression, like an alcoholic or drug addict, the recovery becomes a constant, never ending, life long process. It was a process that I desperately needed to begin.

I yearned for a game of Scrabble. I thought about Topher and his writings. I contemplated the words of his manuscript, and I wondered how he was doing. Our letters were few and far between, but we shared when we could. He was still in rehab, but he had moved to Cirque Lodge in Colorado. He was finally using his money on something other than drugs and alcohol. At any rate, I pondered if his recovery had progressed further than mine.

A part of me wished I was back at the University of Utah. At the very least, I couldn't hurt myself there. If Topher had stayed, we could have played Scrabble, wrote, and talked. I thought less about myself when he was around. That always helped me feel better. Thinking about myself less made me think of Jamal. If Jamal was around, I would be able to recover. Giving him my undivided attention always kept my demons at bay. They were both gone though. One was in Colorado, the other was gone forever.

As the thought of recovery, and redemption, raced through my mind, I jammed my fingers into my mouth again. I pressed hard down on my tongue with my fingers and gagged. The taste of sweat resided in my mouth as saliva filled it. Acid started its slow climb from my stomach to my mouth. My esophagus began to burn as I felt warm vomit make its way upwards. I felt the jagged corners of pills move up my throat. As tears streamed down my cheeks, I heaved over and over again. Vomit escaped my mouth as pills began to dive to the bottom of the toilet bowl. The stench encompassed the bathroom and made my nostrils tingle.

I gagged. I shook. I cried. I hugged the porcelain throne. Lying on the bathroom floor, in the most vulnerable of positions, I sobbed. As my skin felt the coldness of the tile, I stared at the ceiling. I wondered why my struggles continued. I had tried to recover. I took my medicine, went to therapy, and wrote constantly. The suddenly overwhelming suicidal thoughts could have been because of the anti-depressants, but I wasn't sure. I was here again, on the brink of killing myself. After crying for quite some time, I finally fell asleep on the bathroom floor.

I had learned one thing from all the pain, the suffering and the attempt to recover. In these moments of utter despair, I tried to concentrate on the positive things in life. The depression weighed those wonderful thoughts down. It fought them. It tarnished them. It attempted to push them aside. Every day, the depression battled with my memories, weakening them, and trivializing my very existence. The depression diminished my memories. It shrunk the positivity and thirst I had for life. The seemingly insurmountable power struggle between depression and life had just begun. It was a battle that would probably be a never ending fight. And, thus far, the dark forces of pain and sorrow were winning the war.

Despite the support of family, and the very few friends that I shared my struggle with, I felt alone. I was a solitary traveler on this journey of sadness. Their support, while appreciated, was met with mixed feelings. My self-esteem was shattered. My self-worth had disappeared. So, their unwavering support was something that I didn't deserve. I didn't earn it. My merits didn't deem me worthy of love.

The darkness of the night was devastating. As I tossed and turned and hurt myself, I thought of dying. My thoughts of death were met with an assortment of feelings. Some were good. Some were bad. All were unhealthy. All were uncontrollable.

Desperately, I tried to keep the dark thoughts at bay. After spending a couple of hours sleeping on that cold floor, I awoke. It was still dark. I rose to my feet slowly and walked to my bed. I sat on the edge of it, cradling my head in my hands. The alarm clock showed 3:15 a.m. in haunting red. I hadn't made it to the light yet. I wondered if I could. I thought of the pills strewn across the floor and bed. Maybe, just maybe, if I took them all...with that thought, I jumped up. Quickly, I grabbed my jacket, an unmarked bottle of pills, and my keys, before running out the front door.

I couldn't be here right now. I could be anywhere else but here. I didn't know where I was going, when I would come back, or if I would come back, but I was going to try and outrun the pain that followed me. It didn't matter where I went, as long as, the sorrow couldn't keep up. As my car came to life, Matchbox Twenty's *3 AM* sounded through my speakers. A voice rang through my ears as it sang "It's 3 a.m., I must be lonely...well I can't help but be scared of it all sometimes..."

Without thinking, I found myself driving to the cemetery where Jamal was buried. Maybe I didn't have to be alone. As I parked the car, I wondered what it would be like if he was still alive. I walked and walked, my heart heavy, for the loss of such an amazing boy. Finally, using the light of my cell phone, I found the stone that marked his final resting place.

There I sat.

There I cried.

There I apologized.

There I said goodbye.

There I left an unmarked bottle of pills.

The night is the hardest time to be alive
and 4 a.m. knows all my secrets.
- Poppy Z. Brite

Chapter Ten: Jamal...

Fear numbs the blessing of being alive.
- Patricia, Jamal's mother

My hands shook as I grasped the steering wheel. I squeezed the wheel tightly as a loud sob escaped my body. I punched the passenger seat next to me. I felt so consumed with anger, so full of hate. I was so confused, and I yearned to go back for the pills I had left. I wanted it all to end. I wanted to be in the ground. As that thought crossed my mind, I thought about my time with Jamal and the first day we met...

The swamp cooler struggled valiantly to keep the large gym from becoming an unbearable, sweltering sauna. Sweat trickled from my bald head as I continued my trip around the world. A young African American boy, for the second consecutive day, sat quietly on the bleachers. Cautiously, he watched me from a distance. His head was bald like mine, and he ran his hands back and forth feeling the smoothness of his skin. He was mesmerized. I wasn't sure if it was due to the softness of his skin or the accuracy at which my shots tickled the net. After sinking a step-back three, I looked in his direction. My eyes caught his as he smiled. I winked and smiled back at him, but he immediately hung his head. Shyly, he refused to make eye contact, but when I continued shooting, he couldn't resist the desire to watch.

Using the glass backboard, I banked in my final shot, completing my trip around the world without a single miss. It had been quite some time since I had completed the feat. Actually, it was probably the first time since the horrible concussion that had turned me into something I couldn't understand nor recognize. The feelings that welled up inside my soul could be controlled, at least for now. In time though, I wasn't sure I'd be able to harness them. Recently, I had been overcome with an overwhelming urge to hurt myself, but I had refrained from doing so yet. For now, I used basketball to control those thoughts. It had the ability to make me forget, but the desire to actually play was starting to dwindle.

I slowly made my way over to the bleachers where the young boy still sat. He still avoided eye contact. I carried the coveted Southern Utah University team basketball that I had "borrowed" from my older brother. I tried to spin the ball on my index and middle fingers, but I failed miserably. The young boy giggled as the ball toppled off my fingers. It hit the floor with a thud. Quickly, trying to save face, I dribbled the ball as I pulled my shirt forward. Like an And 1 street baller, I caught the ball inside my shirt. For a moment, it looked like my pregnant belly was growing nicely. The boy laughed as he continued to watch curiously. With my hand, I hit the ball, which sent it spiraling around my back. It eventually left my shirt, bouncing on the floor and into my opposite hand. The young boy was now giving me his undivided attention. He was on the edge of his seat, ready for more.

I laughed. I didn't have any more tricks up my sleeve, but he didn't need to know that. I sat on the bleachers, and I reached down to ensure that my Boys and Girls Club volunteer badge was still attached to my shorts. Until now, my volunteering had done little more than help me improve my free throw percentage by 6%. As I sat there, I dribbled the ball quickly under my legs. I increased the speed of the dribbles until a shy, gentle voice sounded behind me.

"Are you sick like me?"

Startled, I lost the ball. It bounced down the gym floor as I watched. Desperately, I wanted to chase after it, but I was paralyzed. Caught completely off guard, I wasn't sure how to respond. Nervously, I looked up at the young boy, who had quickly made his seat in the spot next to me. With a shaking hand, he touched my freshly shaved head.

He repeated the question, "Are you sick like me?"

As his hand continued to feel the softness of my head, I realized just what he was asking. It now made sense why he sat alone in the bleachers. He couldn't play. He was sick, very sick, and he desperately wanted someone, anyone to be like him. He continued to smile at me, but he was impatiently awaiting my response.

I was at a complete loss for words. My eyes began to fill with tears as I fully realized the tragedy he was facing. I wanted to tell him that I was like him. I wanted to tell him that everything would be okay. I wanted to tell him he would play basketball again. I wanted to lie to him. I couldn't though, I wasn't like him. I didn't know if everything would be okay. I didn't know if he would be able play again. I didn't know anything.

As I looked into the eyes of this poor, sickly boy that I had just met, I wanted to take his pain away. For a moment, I wished

I was like him. I knew I couldn't handle the mountain of challenges facing this young boy, but I wanted to help him through them. I had no idea how to do that, but I desperately longed to try.

He still hadn't broken his stare as he awaited my response. My matching bald head made him wonder if I was facing the same cancer that was ravaging his body. He wondered if the chemo had ruined my hair like it had his. His hand still lightly touched my head as I broke down in tears. He cocked his head to the side and looked at me with a state of utter confusion on his face. He stared at me with an expression that was worth a million words. His look simply said..."white boys really are crazy."

As I tried to compose myself, he patted my back softly. I still didn't know what to say, so I just shook my head. I explained to him that I suffered from a receding hair line, male pattern baldness, and just bad genes when it came to hair. However, the shape of my head was outstanding, and it needed to be shared with the world. With that, he laughed. Again, the look that covered his face repeated the same simple message about my craziness.

As I finally gained the courage to ask him about his bald head, a middle aged African-American woman shouted in our direction. "Jamal!" she yelled. In an instant, he took off, never answering my question. I watched as he slowly ran in her direction. I waved to her, but I wasn't ready to actually speak with her. She waved back. Hand in hand, they left the gym together.

I went back out on the floor and started another trip around the world. I was grateful that I still had the strength and energy to play. Although I would feel horrible in a few hours, for now, I was going to okay. Jamal's question lingered in my mind, shadow boxing with my soul. Maybe, I thought, I could help him. I still didn't know how I would accomplish it, but I was determined to find out.

The next day, I was back in the gym. The swamp cooler continued it's never ending battle against the summer heat. Exhausted and covered in sweat, I ran yet another group of youngsters through a game of Dodgeball. As I watched them, I was amazed by the joy that consumed them. I wanted to see Jamal with that joy. It was weird to me that I cared about this boy, the one that I barely knew, so much. I didn't feel pity for him. I felt an overwhelming concern to see happiness radiate from his tattered soul.

For the next week, I didn't see him. I feared the worst. I wondered if his heroic battle could have been lost so fast. I wondered if I missed the one small chance to be part of his life. I had made him smile and laugh that first day, something that appeared to be greatly needed. Still, I may have been too late to make a difference.

I wondered how many days he had sat quietly in the bleachers before I took notice. I wondered how many days I had neglected him before I spoke to him. I wondered how many shots he had watched me make. It didn't matter; I had missed the one shot that I desperately needed to take. I missed the shot at helping the young boy that was climbing an insurmountable mountain alone. I had let him climb without so much as a boost or a word of encouragement, and for that, I felt horribly guilty.

For twelve days, I waited in anticipation. I was hopeful of his return, but I was growing increasingly pessimistic of our chances. As I helped other youths with art projects, sporting events, and nature walks, I felt a void within me. I had convinced myself that helping Jamal would be the only way that I would be making a difference. I wasn't sure why I felt that way, but I hated the fact that I did.

On the thirteenth day, much to my surprise, Jamal and his mother entered the gym. His mother motioned in my direction, and I was immediately nervous. Surely, she had something to say about the "crazy white boy" that had attempted to befriend her son. She sent Jamal to the shuffleboards and sat in the bleachers next to me. As tears streamed down her face, I listened to the horrific struggles facing her young son. He was suffering from CLL, chronic lymphocytic leukemia. The chemotherapy wasn't working. The outlook was bleak, and due to his continued deterioration of health, he could no longer participate in the program.

I patted his mother on the back, searching for the right words. I could have searched for eternity, but the words would never come. They simply didn't exist, not in English or any other language. How do you comfort a mother that knows her boy is dying? How do you comfort a mother that has to watch her boy slowly wither away? How do you comfort a mother that would give anything to take away his pain? How do you comfort a mother that would eagerly sacrifice her own life to save the life of her son? You don't. You can't. It is absolutely impossible. No references to God or Jesus or Heaven change the fact that God is taking her son from her. Nothing will reduce the pain that a mother is feeling when her child is dying before her eyes.

I did the only thing that I knew how to do; I took her in my arms. I took this woman, this mother that I had just met, and I held her tighter than I had ever held anyone before. Sobs of despair left her body as I felt her tears consume my shirt. I hadn't ever experienced death in my family. I had never lost anyone close to me. In a desperate effort to comfort her, I just didn't let go. I just let her cry until she was done.

Once she composed herself as best she could, she proceeded to explain to me that she needed someone to spend 2 days a week with Jamal. While she wanted to spend every waking moment with him, she had to work. She had to provide. She still had to survive. She was teaching me a lesson that I desperately needed to grasp. She didn't have any family or friends that could spend the time with him.

I sat speechless. She could see that I was questioning why she had chosen me. What had I done to be granted the opportunity for such a task? How did this family come to the conclusion that I would be worthy of spending precious hours with him? As I sat there, she watched my wheels turning. I couldn't comprehend what was happening.

Finally, after what seemed like an eternity, I responded. "Yes. But...why me?"

She smiled widely. She pulled a small journal from her purse and showed me an excerpt from thirteen days earlier. It had a sloppy but endearing picture of two bald guys talking in the bleachers. Underneath, Jamal had written in chicken scratch something about me being nice and making a lot of baskets. He thought I was cool, because like him, I was bald.

I wept uncontrollably. Two weeks ago, I had written off my efforts as lackluster, juvenile, and selfish. Today, I was rethinking those thoughts as I evaluated the mission that was just laid out in front of me. On the surface, it seemed so simple. In reality, it was a request to be part of the heartbreak of this family. It was an invitation to take part in their sorrow. It was a summons to accept that he would one day die, but that I could help be part of his final moments.

Overwhelmed, I couldn't respond. I didn't need to though. My looks of extreme excitement and indescribable concern were plastered on my face. She knew that I accepted the mission. For two days a week after that, I became part of Jamal's life. For the rest of my life, Jamal became part of mine. I couldn't have been any happier or more scared of the journey we had begun.

Due to the continued decline in his health, we had to limit our time outside. We would be doused with medical grade hand sanitizer before entering the home. Masks would cover our smiles, but we both knew that they were there. We would play NBA Live, Madden, and Blitz: The League on the Playstation 2 that I bought him. We would talk about basketball, reminding each other that he would play again. One way or the other, whether it was on Earth or in Heaven, he would play again. I shed tears as we spent our days together. I wasn't ready to have to say goodbye.

On the days where his health seemed to be improving, I would wheel him in his wheelchair to the park across the street from his house. There, he would intently watch me play around the world, cheering me on as I didn't miss. For some reason, when he watched, I didn't miss. I wondered if that gave him hope that the impossible was actually possible.

As time progressed, his health continued to get worse. He ended up becoming a resident in the long term wing of the hospital, and we would spend our afternoons watching movies and playing War. I would often deal him every Ace, King, and Queen. He would smile broadly as he destroyed me in battle. When all the cards were his, we would declare him the Emperor of the World. He would proclaim me as one of his loyal subjects and proceed to boss me around for Jell-O cups and ice chips. They were requests that I couldn't complete fast enough.

After 12 weeks with Jamal, his body began to shut down. He struggled. Relief only came in the form of high powered drugs that made him sleep. While his mother worked and he slept, I would sit in a chair beside his bed and read out loud from J.R.R. Tolkein's "The Hobbit". Most times, it seemed the words were falling on deaf ears, but I didn't care. I read to him. I read to him like he was my own. I read to him like everything was going to be okay. I just read...and read...and read.

On a cold night in January, I was awoken by the vibrating of my cell phone. The clock read 2:13 a.m. When I saw the name of the sender, Jamal's mom, I was overcome by tears. I couldn't bring myself to read it. I just held my phone, trembling in fear. After twenty minutes of wishing the message would disappear, I finally opened it. The simple message urged me to come quick. It was time. I cursed myself for being such a coward. I wasted so much time. I rushed to my car and sped off to the hospital.

As I sat at the last stop light before the hospital, my phone started to vibrate incessantly. Cautiously, I ran the red light and pulled into the hospital parking lot. Nervously, I quickly opened my phone Tears filled my eyes as I read the messages. I was too late. Jamal had passed away just moments before I had arrived. His final breaths were taken while I sat at a red light.

I threw my cell phone at the windshield of my car. The cracking thud of plastic sounded throughout the car. The phone broke, and the screen went dark. I sobbed, unable to control myself. I thought about going in to see Jamal's mom, but I was filled with regret. If I hadn't spent 20 minutes sulking, I would have been by his side. I began to resent myself. I laid my head on the steering wheel of my car and cried until I fell asleep.

I awoke a couple of hours later, still being reminded that Jamal was gone. I couldn't go in. I couldn't call or text. Not sure of what to do or how to handle his death, I just left. When I should have comforted his mother, I drove away. I never saw Jamal or his mother again.

A couple days later, I received an invitation to Jamal's funeral. Still bitter, still resenting that he was taken from me, I didn't attend. I refused to celebrate the life of the young man who meant so much to me. To this day, I still regret my actions. I regret how selfish I suddenly became when his death was official. I never spoke to Jamal's mother again, and this is the first time that I have written extensively about him. I blamed myself for years for my inability to be there for his mother and him when they needed me most.

Years later, I wrote his mother a letter. I expressed gratitude and love for her son. I apologized endlessly for my lack of appearance on that fateful night. I never sent it. Instead, on a cold night in January, I threw my words into the fire.

Would you know my name if I saw you in Heaven?
Would it be the same if I saw you in Heaven?
- Eric Clapton and Will Jennings

Chapter Eleven: Hurt...

I hurt myself today
To see if I still feel
I focus on the pain
The only thing that's real.
- Trent Reznor ("Hurt" performed by Johnny Cash*)

A strange, almost mesmerizing power, emanated from the fresh razor blade that I held in my trembling hand. A bright orange flame flickered from the blue candle on my nightstand, and heated the sharp blade to a considerably high temperature. My hand was overcome with a stinging sensation as the blade slow burnt my palm. The blade caught glimmering flashes of light from the television. Those short glimpses of light held my eyes in a trance as I balanced the blade in my fingertips.

The heat on my fingers was extremely painful. Testing the fierceness of the blade, I gently rubbed my index finger along the edge of it. I slowly increased pressure until the blood began to ooze from my skin. The pressure was minimal, and the blade was still quite hot. As I watched the drops of crimson flow, I realized the ferocity of the blade was not to be reckoned with.

I grimaced. The blood ran down my finger, and I stared as it dripped. I gazed as the drops fell in slow motion from my finger to my shorts. The beads of blood grew as they landed, spreading over the area. It was a beautifully terrifying display to witness. The small blade felt extremely heavy. It was awkward to know the power it held over me. Suddenly, I placed it against the top of my wrist. My hand shook wildly. I grabbed chaotically at my wrist to try and calm my mounting nerves. As I held my quivering wrist, the audible, painstakingly horrible sobs started to escape my body. I convulsed with each deep, painful sob. My heart raced frantically. I screamed.

Between my frenzied screams, a guitar strummed beautifully in the background. The music sent chills down my spine. An old, tired voice strained as it began to croon. The powerful, yet weary tone, radiated from my speakers, and filled my empty room. The skillful words escaped the fragile, exhausted voice, but the potency of the lyrics formed goose bumps on my skin. An authoritative, yet elderly legend began, sharing my life...

I hurt myself today
To see if I still feel
I focus on the pain
The only thing that's real. *

I held my right hand in a fist, and I hit myself in the face. My cheek throbbed with each punch. My left hand still clenched the fiery blade. In one quick motion, the blade dug into the top side of my fist. Blood rushed out as I drug the blade through my hand. I gritted my teeth as I set my jaw hard, but after half of an inch, the pain was overwhelming. It consumed my body. I shook from head to toe as a sense of shock began to set in. Through blurry eyes, I watched the wound release more and more of my blood. I sat in a stupor as I stared at the damage I had just done. I took the blade, dripping with my own blood, and dug it into my wrist. Pain coursed through my body. The screams returned. My voice cracked as I shouted madly. I wept uncontrollably. Disgusted, I threw the blood stained blade at the television.

The voice from my speakers continued to share its song of sorrow and heartbreak as tears consumed me. Overcome with desperation and pain, I continued to listen to the words that mesmerized me...

> *The needle tears a hole*
> *The old familiar sting*
> *Try to kill it all away*
> *But I remember everything.*
> *What have I become*
> *My sweetest friend*
> *Everyone I know goes away*
> *In the end.**

It seemed so incredibly ironic, but I was living the lyrics of this tragic song. The tale of regret, fear, and pain was my life. While the needle wasn't present, the razor blade had just torn holes across the top of my hand. The blood continued to gush, a constant reminder of what I had done. I really just wanted to kill away all the pain. The pain that tormented my soul was crushing. I buried my head into my pillow and yelled. I shrieked. In between the intermittent sobs and gasps for breath, the harrowing voice continued its pleas of desperation...

And you could have it all
My empire of dirt
I will let you down
I will make you hurt.

I wear this crown of thorns
Upon my liar's chair
Full of broken thoughts
I cannot repair.

Beneath the stains of time
The feelings disappear
You are someone else
I am still right here. *

The words consumed my soul. I was overcome by the emotions of all that had transpired. No amount of pain, no amount of sorrow would fix my current situation. I was lost, wandering around in my own mind. I combated myself as my unspeakable thoughts were once again getting the best of me. I was full of lies, and they reminded me of the horrible things I had done. My sheets were stained with my own blood, but my appalling feelings of hatred wouldn't disappear.

If I could start again
A million miles away
I would keep myself
*I would find a way.**

I pondered what it would be like to start all over again. I wondered what it would be like to not have these tarnished memories of pain and sorrow. I doubted that I could ever change. I doubted I could ever recover. With that, I screamed. As the beautifully tragic song concluded, I could hear the sound of my heart shattering all over again. Desperately, I pushed my face into my blood stained sheets, and I screamed until I fell asleep.

It had been quite some time since I had slept. The bags under my eyes had darkened considerably. My eyes were always heavy and puffy. Sleep was necessary. For the time being, I appeared to have finally worn myself out enough to get some.

Some nights are made for torture, or reflection, or the savoring
of loneliness.
- Poppy Z. Brite

PART II: A DOG

The great pleasure of a dog is that you may make a fool of yourself with him and not only will he not scold you, but he will make a fool of himself too.

- Samuel Butler

Chapter Twelve: Adoption Day...

He had no particular breed in mind, no unusual requirements.
Except the special sense of mutual recognition that tells dog and
human they have both come to the right place.
- Lloyd Alexander

I was a naturally quiet, gentle person. I would never purposely hurt anyone, but for some reason, I hurt myself. I hurt myself often. And, I hurt myself a lot. I wasn't sure why, but I did. People didn't know it. I hid it from everyone. They would never understand me anyways. My battle was internal. It was intrinsic. It was intense. It was irrational. It was inevitable. For people like me, there was only one immediate escape from the pain.

While everyone else slept, I continued attempting to balance on the tight rope that I had allowed to become my life. More often than not, I would fall as the darkness of the nights continued to overcome me. I would ponder the question of suicide. I didn't always harm myself. There wasn't always a razor blade or pills present. However, I always wondered if my life was worth living. I would ponder that question for hours on end as the tears streamed.

As I struggled to come to terms with myself, the decisions I had made, and the things that I had done, I would start to slowly and painfully wither away. I would try to shrivel up and forget all the good that was in my life. I would allow the overwhelming pain and crushing self-pity to prevail time and time again. I couldn't even begin to understand how or why I continued to allow this to happen. But, it did. It was a never ending cycle.

Life appeared to be on the mend. I was beginning to feel like I was finally in a good spot for true recovery. After moving back to Boulder City, I was alone too much at night. For my sanity and safety, I moved in with Meagan. She helped to control my urges. She helped to protect me from myself.

I had started to come to terms with many of my issues, but I still couldn't shake the pain. I refused to forgive myself. As much as I tried, I just wouldn't allow myself to do it.

The medicine continued to control my thinking, often causing severe moments of suicidal ideations to come and go. Still, my psychiatrist urged me towards recovery. No matter the prodding, I couldn't shake the feelings about the things that I had done. I couldn't sleep, and I hated to eat. For some strange reason, I was always fighting a battle with an overwhelming sadness. It was a foe that refused to give up.

On occasion, I would decide to just stop taking my prescriptions, but the consequences from those decisions were just as bad as taking them. Withdrawing from the medicine would cause me even more issues. During my sleepless nights, I would quietly cry as I wrote in my journal. I would beg and plead for solace. I just wanted peace. Once again, I wanted sleep. I wanted to feel whole again.

Less than three feet away from me was a beautiful, breathtaking young lady that loved me with all of her heart. I wasn't sure why she loved me. I wasn't sure how I got her to love me. I wasn't sure why or how she stayed beside me but she did. I knew I didn't deserve her unconditional love, but for some strange, incomprehensible reason, she loved me. Her absolute, all consuming love was the best thing in my life, but I couldn't seem to just accept the love that was so freely given to me. My troubled mind made me question everything that was good in my life, regardless of whether it made sense or not.

At night, as I scribbled in my journal, I would watch her sleep. She always looked so beautiful. She was so peaceful. While she was dreaming in her own little world, I would look upon her flawless face and smile. Those smiles would be the only ones that came during the difficult nights. As I smiled, I would resent myself. I would resent the man I had become, the coward I was, and the human being that I thought I would end up becoming in the future. I hid my dark scars. I hid my pain. I confided in no one. I just tried to smile. I tried to appear happy, and everyone thought I was on the mend.

The future scared the living hell out of me. Still, I wasn't sure how much more of that "future" I would end up seeing. The nights seemed to drag on, each one longer than the last. Each sunrise seemed harder to make it to. Those horrific urges to harm myself rose up inside me more often. They tormented my soul. I couldn't get them to loosen their deathly grip.

I wasn't sure if I could survive many more nights. I needed something, anything to help me cope. I still wasn't eagerly discussing my issues. I needed someone, something that wouldn't ask me why. I needed to feel an unconditional love that I felt I deserved. I didn't deserve Meagan's unconditional love. I didn't deserve the undying love of my mother and father. I definitely didn't deserve God's eternal love. I desperately needed to earn the love of another, a love that couldn't be manipulated or tarnished. But, where could I find a love like that?

As I pondered if such a love really existed or could exist, at least with me being a part of it, I thought about Carlee. Carlee was my dad's beautiful Golden Retriever. She was a loyal old lady. She loved him with all her heart. She, along with my dad, had saved my life. On that fateful night, when the demons came knocking at my door, and the pills had consumed my body, it was Carlee that prompted my dad to come down the hallway to my room.

She had paced back and forth incessantly, stuck her cold nose under the door, and sniffed madly. She began digging at the carpet and whining frantically. Her actions had awakened my dad, so with her in tow, he had entered the dark empty hallway. The tiny trickles of light from my lamp escaped beneath the doorway of my room. Each one was a spotlight, a desperate plea for help. Needless to say, without Carlee, I wouldn't have survived that night. Her intervention gave me a second chance.

While I couldn't have Carlee as my dog, I pondered what it would be like to have a dog of my very own. I loved dogs. I always had. Maybe, the unconditional love that I could earn from a dog would help me with the recovery process. The path I had to travel was going to be long and dark, and maybe a silent companion, a shadow full of love, would bring me some solace. That thought brought me some much needed peace. And, with that in mind, I finally went to sleep.

I awoke the next morning after a troubled night of sleep. I smiled from ear to ear as I thought about getting a dog. As the sunlight crept in through the blinds, the rays dripping on Meagan's flawless skin, I watched as she slowly opened her eyes. Before she could say anything, I bombarded her with the idea of adopting a dog to share. While she knew of my depression, I hid the scale and depth of my pain. It was a pain that I felt a dog could help cure.

As we eagerly entered the animal shelter in Las Vegas, I was overwhelmed by the decision I was about to make. While my own life spun out of control, held hostage by the desperation in my heart, I was about to become responsible for another life. I had no preferences in mind. I just wanted to save a dog that would hopefully save me.

He sat nervously in the front, a last ditch effort to get him adopted. He was not housed in a kennel, but sat beside an adoption table, shaking as people walked by without giving him a second look. A rope held by a slipknot hung around his skinny neck. His ears, too big for his tiny frame, dwarfed him.

His eyes, full of fear, but mixed with a tinge of hope, looked up into mine. His golden fur was short and beautiful. As my eyes looked down at him, tears started to form. His ribs and spine were on full display. Malnourishment had overcome him. The sickly dog was terrified. As I gazed upon him, I couldn't help but think of myself. He, like me, was broken. He, like me, was hurting. He, like me, needed to be saved. He was me, and I was him.

I stood there in a daze, consumed by my thoughts. I shook. I wasn't sure why. I was nervous, but I didn't know why. The prospects of adopting such a dog hit me hard. I wondered if I would be rejected. Those are the illogical, absolutely irrational thoughts that fill your troubled mind when you are depressed.

Regardless of their validity, they were there. Acceptance was something that I didn't feel I deserved. I wasn't sure if I would find it, not here or anywhere. Still, for my sanity...for my safety...for my very survival, I was here.

His eyes locked intently on me as he peered at me. His dark, hopeful, but sad eyes, gazed deeply at me. It was as if he was looking into my soul. As I watched him, our eyes locked, and a connection was instantly made. In that brief moment, we connected in a way that I didn't think was possible. We were reflections of one another. We were both in a state of utter desperation. We were both trying to escape. We were both yearning for a bond of friendship and unconditional love. We were both fighting to stay alive.

In that moment, a peaceful realization overcame me. It was simple. We needed one another. It was fate. It was as if he were placed here, in this predicament, for me. For a second, I felt guilty as I pondered that thought. What if all his hardships, all his struggles, and all his pain were because of me? What if he was specifically chosen to be broken, like me, so he could help me? What if, in essence, I was responsible for his pain and suffering?

Maybe, his entire life was preparing him to become part of mine.

The common ground that we found ourselves standing on was unstable at best. We teetered and tottered on the edge of a cliff that cast shadows over the inescapable abyss below. We were on the verge of falling, and one wrong move could be catastrophic. It would cause us to fall down into that deep, dark chasm. It was a chasm that both of us had fallen into before. We had fought like hell to still be here, but I wasn't sure if either of us had enough strength to climb out again. Essentially, this was our last chance. But, this time, we would have each other.

Today was to be his final day at the shelter. If today's last ditch efforts were unsuccessful in securing an adoption then he would be euthanized. His life would end. The shelter, like his previous owners already had, were ready to give up on him. To them, he wasn't going to be adopted. His malnourished body scared away prospective owners. His Pit Bull side scared away others. As for the Basenji, most people, including myself, had no idea what type of breed that was. To them, he was a lost cause. Today would determine his fate. He was at the crossroads, and it was up to me to send him one direction or the other.

As all these thoughts ran through my mind, Meagan knelt next to the dog. This was the moment of truth. No matter how much I wanted this dog that represented my brittle soul with his fragile outward appearance, I would have to convince Meagan.

The process of adopting a dog, while more for me, was for both of us. As she reached out towards the dog, his tail started to wag. Rather than waiting for her hand to reach him, he sprang into action. In an instant, he was in her lap. He followed that up with more affection as he proceeded to kiss her face and neck. He refused to stop. He was gentle in his affections. He was not overly hyper. He sat in her lap and just kissed her over and over again. She smiled and giggled as our new found friend was overjoyed.

As I knelt next to him, he nervously climbed out of Meagan's lap and into mine. For a second, he just stared into my eyes. There it was again. We connected. It was as if he was telling me that we both needed this. I knew we both did. Apprehensively, he kissed me before curling up in my lap.

The golden Pit Bull/Basenji mix was severely underweight. Recently, his life had been extremely hard. In prime physical condition, he would be upwards of 50 pounds. As he sat in my lap now, he was lucky to be 20 pounds. The malnourishment allowed his fragile ribs and spine to be on full display. As I ran my hand softly along his sides, I could feel the bones. His ribs, his spine, his hips...each bone exposed. I wondered why someone had done this to him.

How could someone harm him? He was so little, so delicate, so in need of love. As I reached out to pet him, I caught a glimpse of the scars on my hand and wrist. Inside, I was so little, so delicate, so in need of love.

As we prepared to fill out paperwork to bring him home with us, the adoption consultant explained to us that he had been found in the middle of the desert. His previous owners had left him for dead. He had struggled to survive in the intense summer heat, and the pounds just fell off him. The lack of food and water, and the pain of abandonment were about to overcome him when he was rescued.

A clumsy yellow lab and his teenage companions found him. Initially they thought he was dead, but after further investigation, they realized he was barely hanging on. Like me, he was rescued by a concerned wagging tail.

He was transported to a local vet, who seeing him in his state of desperation, thought twice about saving his life. The malnourishment, the dehydration, and the broken heart might have been too much to overcome. But, like me, he somehow beat the odds and survived. After a few days, he ended up, like me, in a facility of his own. He became the newest member of the animal shelter.

He had been adopted once before. It lasted a week before the family brought him back to the shelter. They said he was unable to be trained. Supposedly, he was unruly and mean. On his return trip, he spent weeks waiting. He watched as he was passed over again and again. Ultimately, it only became a matter of time. He was not a popular attraction, and his chances of being adopted were dwindling. In time, he would become disposable as the cost of keeping him alive would be too much.

He sat on the brink. He was on the precipice of death. Like an inmate on death row, all he had left to enjoy was his last meal.

In that moment, as I watched him, tears welled up in my eyes. He was here for a reason, and that reason was me.

He followed closely at my side as we crossed the parking lot. It was official. The dog that was considered unadoptable; unable to be trained, malnourished, and hours away from being euthanized was mine. I had saved him, but the real question remained unanswered; would he save me?

With a slight wag, his tail swished from side to side. He trotted beside me with a nervous apprehension. His eyes seemed hopeful, but he was definitely scared. His fears were only matched by my own. The fear of possible disappointment consumed us both.

I smiled as the setting sun began to work its beautiful magic. It started its slow descent, casting our shadows on the dirty pavement in front of us. A wonderful picture was painted. There we were, side by side. Boy and dog.

As our shadows proceeded, slowly escaping the darkness, I thought about how we were soiled like the pavement. Our shadows were trying to escape from the grittiness as we fought the hopelessness of life. It was a scary reminder, but this time, it made me smile. Sometimes, the shadows are the only things that remind us of the beauty of the light.

It was time for hope. It was time for recovery. It was time for love. It was time for Life with Ziggy.

We can cure physical diseases with medicine, but the only cure for loneliness, despair, and hopelessness is love. There are many in the world who are dying for a piece of bread, but there are many more dying for a little love.
- Mother Teresa

Pictures...

*I've learned that good-byes will always hurt, pictures will never
replace having been there, memories good and bad will bring
tears, and words can never replace feelings.*

- *Unknown*

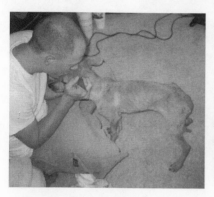 

**Ziggy's Adoption Day - A life of neglect and abuse left
him severely underweight. After being left for dead in
the middle of the desert, he fought to survive.**

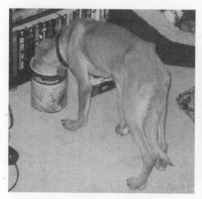 

**Ziggy helping himself
to some ice cream.**

Ziggy and I

Meagan and Ziggy

Ziggy

ZIGGY: THE DOG WHO SAVED MY LIFE

Chapter Thirteen: A New Lease on Life...

Don't start your day with the broken pieces of yesterday. Every morning we wake up is the first day of the rest of our life.
- Unknown

Today was different. Today was a brand new day. It was to be the first day of the rest of my life, or at least that is what I was hoping for. Cliché as that might sound, it was true. After all, I was in desperate need of changes, and I finally felt that I was ready for them. I had put them off for so long, but now I was beginning to hope. For the first time in quite a while, I was eager to let hope consume me.

I stretched and rubbed the sleep from my eyes. The early morning rays of sunlight leaked in through the bedroom window. Rising early had become a common occurrence for me since the depression had set in. For me, I couldn't sleep the day away. While I always yearned to sleep longer, once my mind started turning, there was no chance of me catching any more zzz's.

As I looked around the room, I noticed Ziggy sleeping peacefully in his bed. He had overtaken one corner of the room. I, for the first time in months, slept soundly for the entire length of the night. Even though I didn't sleep in, sleeping through the night was a real victory for me. It was weird that it happened on Ziggy's first night with me. It might have been his presence that calmed me down, or maybe it was just the fact that I was completely wiped out. Maybe it had all finally caught up with me. Either way, I slept.

As I watched Ziggy sleep, I thought about how amazingly ironic it was that I felt that a decision seemingly so small could ultimately change my life. It's true that every decision you make, even the insignificant ones, have some impact on your life. But, could this small decision really change me? Could it cure me? Could it save me? I wasn't sure, but I was hoping that this one decision, the decision to adopt Ziggy, would be one of those life changing ones.

Less than 12 hours earlier, we had made the decision to bring Ziggy into our lives. The small, unhealthy dog was nervous and shy. His eyes, while full of hope, were also consumed by fear. He was unsure of us. He was unsure of himself. His uncertainty equally mirrored mine. His nervousness was only matched by mine. His vulnerabilities were my vulnerabilities. Before Ziggy and I knew one another, we were like one another.

The night before, as we drove home, he sat shaking uncontrollably in Meagan's lap. His oversized ears perked up nervously at every single sound. He trembled furiously with each bump of the car. He was absolutely terrified. The only cure for his nervousness was Fritos. Meagan began to share her bag of Fritos with him, and he eagerly accepted. As Meagan shared chip after chip with our new friend, he slowly began to calm down.

The simple corn chip worked for him. He quickly became her "Rito Partner". When she shared, the shaking slowed, and he began to relax. As he relaxed, he curled tightly up in Meagan's lap and slept soundly.

As we approached our home, Ziggy Marley's "True to Myself" started to play throughout the car. The catchy tune is one of my all time favorites, so I cranked up the volume. As soon as that first uniquely upbeat note hit, Ziggy stood up and began shaking his tail furiously. Suddenly, he was so excited. With a wild frenzy, he kissed Meagan on the face over and over again. Then, without apprehension or warning, he tried to climb into my lap. His tail, still wagging, hit Meagan continuously. We laughed at this silly dog's curious actions. His response brought us to the conclusion that we should name him Ziggy. It was an easy decision. The name fit him. The song seemed to fit us, and our new mission of recovery. It was time for Ziggy to make me be "True to Myself". Eventually, I would have to face the truth anyways. The sooner I could do it, the better, especially with him by my side.

I left Ziggy and Meagan sleeping peacefully in their beds. I was envious of their ability to sleep in, but the early mornings did allow me time to think. I thought about what changes I could make. The overwhelming challenge of trying to take depression on as a whole was truly disheartening. I knew I had to take it one day at a time, but that seemed like such a long time to deal with the crushingly powerful feelings that consumed me. The brain, more than the heart, was my biggest detractor. My thoughts continually urged negativity.

In times of quiet, there was no telling how my mind would react. The silence of the night, or the quietness of the early morning, could be difficult to make it through. On occasion, my thoughts would lift me up and make me extremely hopeful. Other times, my thoughts would hit me in the face, forcing me down with a devastating drowning force. There was also reality. It was the reality of my situation that I was continually attempting to escape. It was the reality that I was constantly running from. I wasn't sure why, but I was. When one looked at my reality, it was easy to see that my life was pretty awesome. I was dating an absolutely stunning young lady. She was incredibly smart, and she had the most amazing sense of humor. She was caring, loving, and fun. That alone should have been enough for me to stop running, but it wasn't.

I didn't know why I was so scared of love, success, and happiness, but I was. I was terrified of receiving any gift that I didn't feel that I truly deserved. If I hadn't earned it, then I didn't deserve to have it given to me. While I knew these thoughts were ludicrous, I couldn't shake them. I allowed the depression to deflate my self-worth, and hold hostage my ability to accept love. I had planted bricks in my heart, and watered them with my tears, in hopes that walls would grow around it.

When I returned to my room, Meagan was still sleeping. She loved to sleep in whenever possible. She would often stay up very late with me, ensuring that I was alright, despite the fact that it would leave her completely exhausted. I obviously didn't mind that she slept in. She deserved it. Now that Ziggy had come into our lives, I figured weekend mornings would be reserved for us.

With that in mind, I looked around the room, but Ziggy was nowhere to be seen. A sense of desperate panic prevailed over me as I looked for him. He had disappeared in minutes, and although there was really nowhere for him to go, I was still panicking. Anxiety was something I struggled to control, and this moment was proving that it was still a problem. Had my one chance at normalcy and happiness already disappeared?

As I was frantically pacing around our room, I heard a tragically weak whimper originating from the darkness of the closet. The door was slightly open, cracked enough for a seriously malnourished dog to enter through. I tried to picture his skinny frame pushing through the opening. I wondered if it had hurt when his exposed ribs rubbed against the wall. I wondered how sensitive his fragile body was to the touch. I had noticed when he laid down yesterday that he had whined in pain. When he did, I was instantly extremely upset with those horrible human beings that had tragically harmed him.

The evening before, when I had finally laid down to go to sleep, Ziggy had paced uncomfortably back and forth for quite some time prior to final resting his weary head. He had been so nervous. His entire body shook with fear. I had tried to comfort him, but my touches only made him more nervous. Tears started to form as I felt his pain. As my shaking hand ran slowly over his bony spine, I cried. He didn't want me to touch him, and while I knew it was going to take time for him to accept me, the rejection hurt. The fear of rejection was the only thing that had made me apprehensive to adopt the malnourished pup in the first place.

When Ziggy finally made his way to his new bed, he cowered in the corner, not yet willing to lie down. He hung his head low, continuing to shake. Despite the rejection I felt, my concerns were not the issue. His current state was horribly heartbreaking to watch. His fear of the night reminded me of myself. At least I could understand what was occurring. His situation was all new to him. It was a dramatic change. While those changes were widely positive for him, the new environment, the new people, and his horrific memories made the situation difficult for him to deal with.

As I looked for him, I thought about how scared he must be. Now that he was awake, the fear was probably returning, consuming his delicate soul. As the cries continued from the closet, I apprehensively crawled towards the opening in the closet doors. I didn't want to scare him, but I was eager to comfort my new friend. I hoped that my attempts at comfort would go better than last night. My desire to help him was intense. After all, I had been in his position before, alone, and scared.

The gold track of the closet doors shimmered as the light reflected off of it. The intense smell of urine radiated from the trough. As I distraughtly peered inside, there sat a tremblingly Ziggy. He cowered in the darkness of the back corner. His head hung low as he refused to make eye contact with me. He was visibly afraid and shaking dramatically. As I calmly called out to him, he laid down on his belly, still refusing to look up at me. He started to crawl towards me, slowly sliding his tiny body across the floor. As he did, the smell of urine intensified. Due to his mounting fear, he could no longer control his bladder. He had begun to urinate all over himself. This caused him to hang his head even lower. He was absolutely ashamed.

As he neared me, my movements scared him, and he darted out of the closet as fast he could. He ducked his head, anticipating a beating as he scooted by. His bony body swerved, and he squeezed swiftly under the bed. I watched as he slid his emaciated frame to the very back corner. As he did, the most horrific whimpers escaped his body. As I watched him, shaking in the corner, I couldn't stop the tears from forming.

He was me. It was that simple. My emotions would have been in disarray for any dog in this predicament, but the constant reminder of me, in him, was absolutely devastating. Just a couple nights earlier, I had sat in the corner of the bathroom and whimpered. I had been terrified as I held a bottle of pills. While I couldn't remember if I had urinated on the floor at that time, I couldn't guarantee you that I hadn't done it in the past. I could relate to his behavior. His resistance to accept, his resistance to trust, his overwhelming fear...it was nothing new to me.

He refused to trust anyone. He had been harmed too many times to accept that someone was trying to help him. Even if someone was actually helping him now, I am sure he wondered how long it could possibly last. I tried to coax him out of his hiding spot, but I was totally unsuccessful. This time, he didn't even attempt to move towards me. He had accepted the deep, dark corner of the bedroom, under the bed, as his hiding place.

When Meagan tried to convince him to come out, the results were the same. The terrified animal would just whimper more traumatically each time we tried. I had no idea what to do. I was dancing on that delicate line between caring and smothering. I desperately wanted to help him, which would also help me, but I just didn't know how.

In a last ditch effort, my final hope for a peaceful resolution, resided in the small amount of leftover Fritos from yesterday's trip home. As I tossed a couple of chips his way, he flinched. It broke my heart to think of the abuse that this poor dog had suffered. Every motion, no matter how small, would make him flinch. When his snout caught the aroma of those wonderful, salty snacks, his tail finally began to wag. It was the first positive reaction of the morning.

With the continuous thud of that wagging tail sounding in the background, he followed the trail of Fritos out from under the tiny space. His love of Fritos outweighed the fear which consumed him. He loved the chips so much that he ended up in my lap. He happily crunched chip after chip. After a few chips, he postured upwards, and kissed my cheek cautiously. His simple action made me smile. He continued to cower in my lap. He still shook, but he was in my lap, and as I cried for him, that was all that mattered.

The issues that presented themselves with this mistreated animal would be hard to overcome. Would he forgive people, and accept a second chance? Like me, he had some decisions to make. Would I forgive myself, and accept a second chance? I guess patience was in order for both of us. Only time would tell if we would crumble and fall, or if we would grow and recover. There was a small glimmer of hope for both of us, and I wondered if that was enough.

I found myself realizing that I could only feed Ziggy so many bags of Fritos. I secretly wished that Fritos would have the same relaxing impact on me. While I had experimented with Original, Chili Cheese, and Cool Ranch, I was unsuccessful. I tried two bags of each for good measure. It might have been three of the Chili Cheese, but I had to be sure. If they worked for Ziggy, maybe they would eventually work for me.

Sometimes, comfort can be found in the smallest and simplest of things. As human beings, we tend to make the discovery of comfort much more difficult than it needs to be. For Ziggy, Fritos were comfort. For me, I desperately hoped Ziggy would be my comfort.

As Ziggy sat in my lap, still shaking, even after polishing off yet more Fritos, I began to wonder if our new lease on life was really worth attempting. Were we too broken? Like an old car, were we really worth fixing? Was the damage irreparable? I guess only time would be able to answer that question, but as Ziggy snuggled in my lap, for the first time in a long time, I was alright with waiting to find out.

...One touch, one glance, one sound can make a difference in the life of someone who feels they mean nothing in this world.
- Make a Sound

Chapter Fourteen: Unexpected Disappointment...

Disappointment is often the salt of life.
- Theodore Parker

I sat on the back porch. I ate my breakfast as I enjoyed the early morning sun. A light breeze caused leaves to flutter, dancing with each gust. Somewhere, a couple of birds chirped in the trees. Quietly, I sat there, watching Ziggy venture cautiously around the backyard. He nervously crept through the bushes that covered the area. From time to time, he would skittishly jump to one side, and his tail would instantly tuck between his legs.

He was always on edge. His surroundings terrified him. He could often be found cowering in corners or hiding in closets. When people approached him, he would hang his hand. When men approached him, he would flinch and whine. When he got scared enough, he would lose his bladder, which brought upon him even more shame and fear.

A deep, impatient part of my heart was being to regret my choice to adopt Ziggy. I wondered if this decision, like all my others, was just another big mistake. Maybe the apprehension I had felt at the shelter was warranted. Maybe our connection was just in my imagination. Maybe I had forced my head to believe what my heart wanted. I was so desperate for companionship and unconditional love, I had falsely fashioned a bond that wasn't really there. I had imagined a recovery with Ziggy that couldn't really happen.

As I watched him, I cursed at myself. For the past two weeks, we had struggled with one another. It was becoming increasingly more difficult for me to feel optimistic about our situation. Since that first morning, the one where the Fritos convinced him to sit on my lap, he had avoided me. He would hide for me, run from me, and cower if I ever got too close. He refused to come to me or let me pet him.

The evening before, I crept to his bed as he slept. Lightly, I petted his ears. They were so soft. Tenderly, I patted his head, and I smiled as his eyes started to open. Immediately after he recognized me, a horrific whimper escaped his fragile body. He bolted from his bed, making his getaway to the corner of the open closet. The scent of urine hung in the air. The carpet was wet with streaks of piss. In the corner, he cowered. In the corner, he cried. In the corner, he stayed.

I buried my head in my heads, refusing to pursue him. I was frustrated, disappointed, and heartbroken. I cursed myself for thinking that my plan would work. We were too broken to come together. With that thought, I wiped the tears that had begun to form in my eyes, picked up my keys, and stormed out of the house.

I was consumed with anger. I was so disappointed with Ziggy's inability to accept me. He had easily accepted Meagan. He loved her more and more every single day. He would cuddle with her on the couch. He would sleep next to her in bed. He would kiss her. He would listen to her.

When it came to me, he would hide. He would cringe. He would whine. He would run away. He would ignore me.

I was frustrated, and I was scared. My plan of recovery wasn't even close to working. My plan, the one I thought I had planned to perfection, was failing horribly. He was my last hope, and if this didn't work, I wasn't sure how I would handle it. I wasn't sure what would happen to me.

That night, when I arrived home, I found Meagan and Ziggy asleep, snuggled closely in bed. As I looked at them, I smiled, but I was envious of the relationship they had. The ease at which they had accepted one another was something that I deeply resented. Selfishly, deep inside of me, I hated it. I hated myself for feeling the way I did, but he was supposed to be my dog.

I had saved him. Didn't he know that? He was supposed to save me. Didn't he know that? He was me, and I was him. Didn't he know that?

That night, I pouted. I curled up on the couch, not quite understanding the anger that was filling my body. I should have been happy that Ziggy had bonded with Meagan. I should have been happy that he was trying, but I wasn't. I was disappointed. I was disappointed in him. I was disappointed in me. I was disappointed in progress.

I slept on the couch, accepting the fact that I was alone.

The next morning, as I watched him, scurrying around the backyard, I felt hopeless. He was so tiny, so skinny, and so scared. He would whimper at rocks, trees, and birds. Everything scared him. I began to realize that he really was like me. I felt like a hypocrite for being so anger with him. Like him, I was refusing to accept the love that was so generously given to me. Like him, I was scared of everything. Like him, I needed time, patience, and unconditional love.

The devastating, crushing fear that consumed him was warranted. After all, he had been beaten, neglected, and left for dead. A man had done all this to him, so his reluctance to accept me had to be understood. His fear of men, and his current fear of me, had helped drive him into Meagan's loving arms. Maybe, in time, he would be driven into my loving arms as well.

My thoughts were interrupted by a loud whimper. Ziggy skittishly scampered out of the bushes, rushing to my side. As he approached, he screeched to a halt. He looked up at me as he shook. Then, he looked back at the bushes. I could see that he wanted to come to me, but he was too scared. Despite my pleas, he utterly rejected the idea of being close to me.

He sat halfway between the bushes and me. Nervous of both possibilities, he began to urinate on himself. I was devastated by the overwhelming fear that radiated from his battered body. As I watched him, I was reminded of that poor girl from rehab. The same fear had radiated from her battered and scarred body. I began to cry as I was reminded of all those people struggling; the ones broken, the ones hurting, the ones like Ziggy, and the ones like me.

Ziggy sat on the concrete, still nervously exchanging glances with the bush and me. I watched him, wishing I could just take him into my arms. Doing so, however, would result in more whimpers, more shaking, and more urine. We both just sat, eyes locked on one another.

Suddenly, a loud fart escaped from Ziggy. It echoed loudly off the concrete. His body jumped at the noise. He immediately turned to face the ground where his rear end had just been. He began to growl, pawing at the ground as he did. He spun in a circle and barked at the ground. When he barked, it surprised him, scaring him even more. Basenjis rarely, if ever, bark, and when he did, he was terrified of it. The fur on his back and neck stood on end. He looked at me, questioning where the sounds, both the fart and the bark, came from. All I could do was laugh. Even farts scared this curious little dog.

Ziggy had urinated on himself again. The poor dog couldn't control it. Whenever he was scared, he lost it. As he followed, cautiously behind me, I knew I had to bathe him, but I didn't know how he'd handle it. As we approached the bathroom, I slowly turned, surprising him as I did. Quickly, I picked him up. He struggled, whined, and urinated. I whispered to him, desperately hoping to calm him down. I lightly scratched his neck, but he continued thrashing about, scratching my arms and face in the process. Still, I held him close, feeling his warm urine against my body.

As I started the water, I softly set him inside the tub. He immediately began trying to escape. He whined as I held him inside the tub. He shook as the warm water covered his golden fur. As I softly ran my hands over his fur, his fear grew. The mounting fear that consumed him forced him to urinate again. As he did, his bowels were also released. The scent of urine and feces penetrated the air. Ziggy hung his head as I stared in disbelief. In an instant, he jumped out of the tub and ran out of the bathroom.

Soaking wet, he rushed through the house. He jumped on the couch and shook. He dropped to the ground, rubbing his wet fur against the carpet. He ran back to the bathroom door, and he growled at me. I sat there, not knowing what to do. As I looked at him, he took off into our room. He took refuge in the closet, whimpering as he did. Once again, I left him there.

Disappointed, I began cleaning the bathroom as tears fell from my eyes.

Ziggy was not ready for me to be a major part of his life. I doubted that I ever could ever play a positive role in it. Part of me was ready to give up on this journey that we had once eagerly begun. It was becoming horribly frustrating and utterly heartbreaking. It was a tragic waste of time.

Ziggy spent much of the remaining day sleeping in the closet until Meagan returned. Once she was back, he was glued to her side. He was in sync with her shadow, closely following her wherever she went. That night, he slept right beside her.

The next morning, we took Ziggy to see the horses. In the car, he sat eagerly on Meagan's lap, his tail wagging as he gazed out the window. As we entered the corrals, he began to whine excitedly. He scratched at the window eagerly. He wanted out of the car as quickly as possible.

When Meagan opened the door, he pranced enthusiastically to the fence and began digging at the base of it. As a large brown horse approached him, his tail began to wag furiously from side to side. He stood on his hind legs, attempting to get closer to the large animal's face. Meagan scooped him up in her arms, and she held him closer to the horse. The horse sniffed, and Ziggy kissed him back.

His love for horses was quite remarkable. He would stay at the corrals for as long as we would let him. As we walked around, letting him take in all the horses in the area, he was overjoyed. He would prance from side to side, sniffing all the scents the ground had to offer. In those moments, while he still kept his distance, I noticed he was less skittish. He was more carefree and happy.

As we rounded a corner, chickens could be heard scurrying about. They clucked. They squawked. When Ziggy heard them, he took off. He ran full speed ahead as the chickens scattered wildly. He turned, looking proudly at Meagan. When he did, a group of chickens started to come up behind him. They tried to peck at him. As the group chased him, he was instantly terrified.

The chickens pursued him relentlessly, pushing him up against the fence. He cowered, afraid of what they might do to him. I called for him, screaming his name. As the chickens closed in, he bounded off in my direction. He plowed through any chickens in his way. He rushed past Meagan and jumped into my waiting arms. As I scooped him up, he began licking my face. He was shaking, but his tail was wagging as he kissed me. I held him close. He didn't cower, he didn't hesitate, and he didn't lose his bladder. He laid his head on my shoulder as tears formed in my eyes.

For the first time since the beginning, he eagerly came to me. He had made his home in my arms. He had let me pet him, love him, and rescue him. It was a victory that I desperately needed. It was a milestone in our young relationship that could possibly change our future. In that moment, he accepted me.

I carried Ziggy, in my arms, back to the car. He nuzzled my neck and kissed my cheek. When I placed him softly in Meagan's lap, he looked back at me with those eyes full of love. As we stared at one another, that connection, the one from the shelter, returned. He was my dog, and I was his person. We were meant to end up together.

While driving home, Ziggy continuously climbed into my lap and kissed my face. I held back tears as I realized that a small change had just occurred in both of us. Despite all our flaws and insecurities, maybe we could beat the odds. Maybe two broken pieces could be united with the hope of being repaired.

That night, as I sat alone on the couch, writing in my journal, I cautiously reminded myself to not get overly excited about today's victory. While Ziggy and I had appeared to take a big step forward, we could just as easily take three steps backwards. I still wasn't ready to accept that we were on the right track.

I sat alone in the dim light, writing about how I yearned to heal him. I figured that if I did, the process might heal me as well. I began to cry as I thought about all the horrible things I had done to myself. I had hurt myself so many times, and I was afraid that I would never stop.

Tears fell from my eyes and landed on the paper below. I watched as the ink smeared. Through blurry eyes, I could see Ziggy coming out of the bedroom. I smiled, wiping the tears from my face. Still, they continued to fall. He looked up at me, concerned and intrigued. I called his name, badly hoping that he would come to me. His large ears, still dwarfing his body, perked up when he heard his name. His tail began to wag, and he rushed to me. He jumped onto the couch, immediately finding a place in my lap. He licked my face wildly, resting his paws on my shoulders. I embraced him and let his love wash over me.

It was a moment that I will never forget. He showered me with his love. As I held him, I sobbed uncontrollably. He caught my tears of relief as he snuggled in my arms.

His ears were often the first thing to catch my tears.
- Elizabeth Barrett Browning

Chapter Fifteen: Dead Birds & Cold Swims...

A single event can awaken within us a stranger totally unknown to us. To live is to be slowly born.
- Antoine de Saint-Exupery

The sun seemed to shine a little brighter, the days seemed to be a little lighter, and the nights weren't nearly as scary. While I still had my moments of doubt, intense feelings of inadequacy, and my regrets, happiness was starting to radiate from within my soul. When the dark times started to rise up, Ziggy was always right there by my side. Although it had only been a few weeks since Ziggy had accepted me, I could already feel the changes happening within me. The changes were occurring within Ziggy as well, as he was adjusting to life with me. When those dark, difficult nights arose, we would sit up together, in the dark, eating Fritos.

Ziggy had struggled through so many rough patches in his life. He had been beaten, malnourished, abandoned, and left for dead. When we started spending time together, he was transformed back into an innocent, fun, and loving puppy. Part of me secretly resented the fact that he adjusted so easily. Maybe it wasn't easy for him, but he sure made it look that way. Still, I was extremely happy to see his renewed vigor and thirst for life. His changes were rubbing off on me. It may have been in small doses, but it was happening.

On occasion, when Meagan was still sleeping on those early Saturday mornings, Ziggy and I would go for a run. I would lace up my Asics, grab the dog leash, and after sharing a couple Fritos, we would hit the pavement. In the early hours of the morning, as the sun was still on the rise, we would start our bonding ritual. It was quiet, and the rest of the world seemed to still be fast asleep. It was relaxing to watch the world wake up. As the morning sun rose, I found myself thankful that I had one more day. I had one more chance to make things right.

Ziggy would trot by my side, and as the sun hit our backs, our shadows would move in unison on the concrete before us. It was an uplifting sight for me. We moved in harmony...one foot, one paw...always together. Even though our shadows exposed our goofiness, we didn't care how ridiculous we looked. Our shadows revealed our ears, the ones that were way too big for our heads. They would cast their own shadows over anything that got in our way. It didn't matter though, like everything else we did, at least we were doing it together.

As we ran along our usual route, I would allow Ziggy to forget the leash. After all, he never strayed far from my side. The dog that was considered impossible to be trained would listen to my every command. He would follow my lead, most of the time anyways. There was only one thing that would set Ziggy off. There was only one thing that would make him throw caution, commands, and common sense to the wind. When Ziggy saw a flock of birds, he would lose his damn mind. He would be overcome with an almost toxic mixture of overwhelming joy and unruly chaos.

As our morning jog entered the park, he would instantly take off like a rocket. He would lower his head, and accelerate his body full speed ahead. In wild anticipation, he would run rampant across the field in a hopeful search of whatever flocks of birds he could find. Once he made his glorious discovery, he would run through the middle of the flock, sending the birds scattering in every direction. His tail would wag wildly as he was filled with an indescribable joy.

When the flock was brave enough to make another patch of grass their landing spot, he would find them again. This practice would occur as many times as the birds would allow it. Again and again, they would scatter in the air only to land so Ziggy could repeat the process. He would continually rush the flock, sometimes rushing the birds so fast that they would collide with him, or each other, as they attempted to take off in a hurry.

In these special moments of chaos, fur, and feathers, that malnourished, terrified puppy, the one that had started to fatten up and develop some courage, would have a twinkle in his eye that made me smile. It was like watching a child play with an empty box. The joy found in the smallest of things was truly remarkable. His actions reminded me of the simple joys that were everywhere in life. As adults, at some point, we forget those little, simple things that make life so much fun. Empty boxes and flocks of birds can be more entertaining than one could ever imagine. Ziggy was giving me those moments of pure joy that I desperately needed. As I watched him chase the flocks of birds, sending them spiraling into chaos, I was happy.

His unrivaled love for birds made the trips to the park that much more exciting. As I ran through the grass attempting to keep up with him, although I had no chance of actual doing so, I would forget about the pain of days gone by. For a short time, my scars would be temporarily erased. I would think of happiness, light, and my new love of life, which was something I never did enough of. I didn't do enough of it before the depression. I definitely didn't do enough of it during. And, although the depression wasn't even close to gone, it was something that I was finally starting to do more of now. It was because of Ziggy, and I was appreciative of it.

On one particular morning, as we chased the flocks of birds together, Ziggy suddenly disappeared down a small grassy hill into a grove of trees. For a few short moments, he was out of my direct line of sight. For the first time since our relationship began, I wasn't worried about him. We had bonded, and he would be back. Exhausted from our running, and tired from causing chaos, I took a moment to just lie in the grass. I watched the clouds float effortlessly throughout the beautiful blue sky. Unlike that tragic night that started our story, I was finally able to enjoy the beauty of the world again. Ziggy was helping that come back to me. It was slow, but it was occurring.

As I smiled upwards at the heavens, I heard the familiar panting of my best friend. He was returning, rushing towards me. I laid there, and I closed my eyes tightly, expecting an attack. Normally, in instances like this, Ziggy would come at me and jump on my chest. He would be overwhelmed with excitement and energy. He would attack me with a never ending swarm of slobbery and sloppy kisses. So, expecting this, I laid there, and braced for his impending impact. I waited, but there was none. Absolutely nothing! Still, I kept my eyes closed as I heard him standing over me. I waited in eager anticipation. I knew I wouldn't have to wait long, because in a minute he would attack me with love.

Suddenly, my face was hit by a slobbery wet, stinky mess of something awful. I shouted and jumped up immediately. It wasn't the kisses from my best friend. It couldn't have been. Even his dog breath couldn't have smelt that rank. My shrieks, high pitched and slightly disturbing, probably would have embarrassed the second grade girls at the local elementary school, but I didn't care. Whatever had touched my face had given me a serious cause of the heebie geebies. While I wasn't exactly sure what the heebie geebies were, I definitely had them now.

I glanced down quickly to see the carcass of an extremely large black crow that now sat where my head once did. I gagged as I stared down at it. That nasty lifeless corpse had just been sitting on my face. As I looked at Ziggy, I was so angry. I could feel my blood starting to boil within me. Ziggy just sat there in perfect formation. Tail wagging; he gazed up at me as an overwhelming look of pride and satisfaction formed on his face. He was truly impressed with his actions. In that moment, I guess I was too. Not because he had dropped a big, nasty, dead bird on my face, but because he could drop a big, nasty, dead bird on my face, and still make me smile. As gross as it was, I couldn't help but laugh. While I was pretty sure I had just contracted the bird flu or something else horrible, I couldn't stop smiling. He just had that impact on me, and I was so thankful for that.

I wasn't sure if he had caught and killed the bird or simply found it when he ventured down the hill into that nested grove of trees. Regardless, I didn't care. It made me smile, and that was worth more than anything. Still, I didn't want any more dead birds on my face, so it was time to leave. As we walked to the restrooms so I could wash the dead bird juices off my face, Ziggy spotted a flock of ducks. In an instant, he was off. The ducks scattered attempting to take refuge in the water nearby. Ziggy stopped at the pond's edge, and he began whining incessantly. He paced the shoreline. He stepped a paw in, only to pull it out quickly. He hated the water, but he wanted a duck.

For me, I could do without any more birds, at least for today. Ziggy, on the other hand, gave in. He dove into the water, dog paddling after the ducks. He darted to left, but that one escaped. He jetted to the right, but that one escaped. He was out of his element in the water. Unlike when he was on land, he couldn't keep up with the ducks in the pond. He started to panic, swimming in circles, not sure of which duck to try and catch. As he continued to try and catch the ducks, he started to fatigue. I yelled for him to swim to the shoreline, but he was confused. He started to struggle to keep his head above water. Between the fatigue and the cold, confusion was setting in.

I started to panic. I yelled for him over and over again. My shouting seemed to confuse him more. His head started to sink again as he fought to keep his snout above water. The dog, who had survived everything life could throw at him, couldn't have his life end like this. No amount of pleading was working. He just continued to swim in misguided circles. He was absolutely clueless as to where he should go. His struggles intensified as he began to panic. I trembled as I watched him start to sink.

Suddenly, without thinking, I quickly kicked off my running shoes and jumped in the water after him. There I was, on a cool morning in early March, swimming in some stinky, nasty, freezing cold water. The sun was still on the rise, and I was freezing my balls off. Ziggy, on the other hand, had already had his removed. Balls or no balls, it was freaking cold.

I am pretty sure that it was quite the sight to behold for the other early morning runners visiting the park. Although my current situation was not ideal, I couldn't help but smile as I thought about the laughter coming from the passing spectators. You had Ziggy, the dog with the massive ears that could easily double as floatation devices, swimming in circles unable to catch the duck of his choice. He was followed by a young man, still skinny and pale, fully clothed and attempting to rescue or chase after him. Neither of us were very strong swimmers. Our weak dog paddles were very similar. For someone, somewhere, it was quite the show.

As I watched my breath escape from my mouth, I shivered. My lips quivered. The water was taking its toll on me as well. As soon as Ziggy saw me approaching, he made a bee line for me. He swam directly into my arms, and when he hit them, he instantly relaxed. I didn't, but he did. I floated on my back, holding him on my chest. My swimming and rescue merit badges were finally coming in handy. His heart was still pounding uncontrollably. As we slowly made our way back to shore, he finally started to calm down.

The water stunk. I stunk. For the second time in less than fifteen minutes, Ziggy had placed me in a truly disgusting predicament. Dead birds and nasty pond water were not my forte, but that was my morning. As I stood on the edge of the pond, shivering in the cool early morning, I just started laughing hysterically. I was laughing so hard that my knees buckled, and I had to sit down. My stomach was hurting from the intense laughter. Well, that and the lack of Fritos.

That morning, for the first time since Topher watched me fall out of my chair, I laughed until I cried. Tears fell from my eyes as I giggled. Ziggy rushed over to me and started licking my cheeks. Then he stopped suddenly, he took two steps, and shook, sending more of that nasty pond water on me. Like the moment earlier, I couldn't help but just smile.

As he returned to my lap, he kissed my face as I grinned. Maybe, just maybe, we were going to be alright after all. Maybe we were not beyond repair. Maybe we were on the mend.

Maybe we could recover. All those maybes weren't even possibilities a couple months ago, but for now, Ziggy was making things possible. Possibilities were new, and while they were not certainties, they were good enough for me.

Ziggy was changing my life. Ziggy was making me forget about my mistakes. He was letting me forget about the anxiety of the future. He was making me live in the present. If that meant a day with dead birds, cold swims, and laughing until I cried, then that was alright by me.

Never could I breathe love if I did not first learn
to inhale a little bit of chaos.
- Christopher Poindexter

Chapter Sixteen: Perfection...

You are imperfect, you are wired for struggle,
but you are worthy of love and belonging.
- Brene Brown

Ziggy made a habit of bringing me dead birds. It was a truly disgusting habit, but it was one that he simply enjoyed bombarding me with. Secretly, I thought he enjoyed seeing me squirm and listening to me shriek. Most times, I would gag when he dropped some unrecognizable corpse on me. My eyes would water. My stomach was, and always has been, incredibly weak. So, when something rank and decaying was given to me, I would lose it.

Dead birds were not the only dead things that he seemed to find. I swear that this dog could track down a dead animal in the cleanliest of places. No matter what excursion we went on, he was bound and determined to make at least one horrific discovery to drop at my feet. Disgusting. Disturbing. Determined. Dependable. That was just Ziggy for you.

His exploits of fetching dead things were notorious. When we went camping, he brought us a dead snake. When we went exploring on Radar Mountain, he brought us a lizard. When we ventured to Lake Mead, he brought us an unrecognizable carcass of something terrible. Our nasty little puppy found dead things everywhere, and he was always so eager to show us his treasures. Countless times, carcasses of something that used to scurry across the ground, swim in the water, or fly in the sky would find their way onto my shoes. There were fish guts, bird juices, and lizard tails just to name a few.

As nasty as this habit was, it was yet another reminder of how simple life can be. Each time, he would stare up at me with an overwhelming look of satisfaction on his face. Pride consumed him. For some strange, inexplicable reason, these instances warmed my recovering heart. Like a confused but proud dad, I would cheer him on, regardless of how nasty his habit was. Well, that was after a painful groan, a disgusted gag, and a shout to drop it. Still, I am pretty sure that there was a sense of pride hidden somewhere in that combination of things. I didn't always show it, but it was there.

For the first time in over a year, I had a full month where I didn't have a single inkling of suicidal ideation. It was the first time, in a long time, that I didn't even think about the possibility of harming myself. The thought of that alone was a success. The realization that I was recovering was now the thing that brought tears to my eyes. It was no longer the darkness of the night, an intense hatred of myself, or the fear of the future that conjured up the tears. It was love; the feeling of happiness, and the realization of recovery, that made them fall.

My last outburst of true sadness, and loneliness, was short lived. In the middle of the night, I sat on the couch, shaking and crying with full bottles of Luvox and Serquel in my hands. There, I pondered ending it all. As I did, Ziggy came wobbling around the corner, his eyes still full of sleep. Confused and tired, he jumped quickly into my lap, and kissed my face before curling up comfortably with me. It was that simple interaction. No desperate attempt to save me before it was too late, just a simple reminder that he was there.

His intuition was spot on. Rather than consume too many pills to count, I tossed the bottles away, and I held him close. I slowly petted his big floppy ears and cried. The cry was a reminder of the strength that I still had left. It was the indescribable strength that he was giving me day by day; the strength that allowed me to continue on.

As the outbursts disappeared, a smile became a more permanent fixture on my face. I had come to accept the fact that I wasn't perfect, nor would I ever be such. I was alright with that, in fact, with that realization came relief. Meagan and I had reached milestone after milestone in our relationship. I was amazed by the ease and grace in which she loved me. It was unbelievable to me that we had made it this far. With all the cards in the deck stacked against us, we had beaten the odds. She had accepted me for who and what I was, and I truly loved her for it.

It would have been so easy for her to leave. She had so many opportunities to wash her hands of me. She didn't. She loved me regardless of my struggles, my insecurities, and my pain. It was truly remarkable. Despite the adversity in our relationship, while everyone else thought we were wrong for one another, we both knew that we were right.

On our nightly walks, we would laugh constantly. We joked. We touched. We kissed. My joy was over the moon. I loved her with all my heart. Between Ziggy and her, I was becoming a new person. I guess I shouldn't say new. I was more like mixing the old with the new. I carried scars, and I always would. As much as

I just wanted to erase them all, I needed them. They were a reminder of what I used to be. They were a reminder of how far I'd come. They were a reminder of how far I could go.

Every night, we would walk Ziggy to the elementary school. In one corner of the playground, amongst the slides and monkey bars, a massive collaboration of crickets would congregate. We would sit on a bench and hold hands as Ziggy excitedly snatched up cricket after cricket. He loved to catch them and there were hundreds for the taking. His tail would swish from side to side often sending the ones behind him flying. He tried to be delicate. He would carefully tap dance around trying to catch as many as possible. He tried not to stomp on any of them, as that would make them unacceptable to consume. It was hilarious to watch.

As we laughed together, I thought about how romantic it was. Yes, I know the backdrop of a big eared Pit-Bull/Basenji mix eating crickets doesn't sound appealing, but if you haven't tried it, you really should. It rivals the tales told in novels by Nicholas Sparks. As we sat there, I would fall in love with her all over again. The full moon shined down, the stars twinkled in the sky, and the dim light from the lamppost danced on our skin. It was as if all this beauty was specifically designed for us. The moon was shinning for her. The stars were twinkling for me. The dim light was probably for Ziggy; otherwise he wouldn't have been able to see his crickets.

As I watched her, giggling at him and smiling at me, I knew with absolutely certainty that she was the love of my life. Love is difficult to explain, and it is different for everyone. Still, I have always found it extremely amusing the way love is depicted in the movies. It is always realized at romantically impossible and unrealistic moments.

In real life, I have never run at full speed through a busy and bustling airport for Meagan, although she has done it for me. She was running late and going to miss her flight though. I have never rushed down a busy city street, dodging traffic just to catch her in the nick of time, although she has done it for me. That was because I took her cell phone. I have never placed countless candles atop a high rise balcony with a breathtaking view of the ocean. Once, however, I tried placing twenty candles in my room, but my pants caught on fire. When the firemen showed up, that was a whole different type of romantic, a romantic that didn't include me.

In reality, a romantic night was holding her hand for so long that our palms got sweaty. While the sweat from our palms mixed, our hearts would beat in unison. While our heats beat in unison, our eyes would lock as we stared longingly into one another's souls. While we stared, butterflies would dance methodically in our stomachs. While the butterflies danced, we would feel like it was the first time again. While we felt like it was the first time, we would kiss. Those kisses, the ones where the moon shined, the stars twinkled, and the dim light danced, all while a puppy caught his buffet of crickets, were the most romantic and memorable of all.

Some may laugh at that notion, but it is true. The most romantic moments are the ones that are neither planned nor executed to perfection. They are those spur of the moment occurrences. The ones you weren't expecting. If your only romantic moments involve dinner, music, and candlelight, then you are doing something wrong. If you introduce a dog, some crickets, and some moonlight, you might be amazed at what happens. I know it definitely worked for me.

As we walked home slowly, hand in hand, with Ziggy trotting slightly ahead of us, I smiled. Life was definitely worth living.

Love was worth diving into head first. Hope and luck were worth believing in. Life was pretty fantastic.

That night, as we shared warm covers and cold toes, a few tears quietly escaped my eyes. They were those welcomed tears of happiness. Just months ago, I had come within an inch of ending my life. I would have missed out on all of this; dead birds, cold swims, and crickets. As her head pressed against my chest, I watched as she fell asleep to the rhythm of my heartbeat. My tears escaped from my eyes and found their way into her beautiful brown hair. I held her close, and I tenderly kissed her cheek. As I did, a cold, wet nose started to nuzzle its way between us.

Ziggy pushed hard, forcing his way between our faces. His soft fur rubbed against my cheek. He aggressively pushed downwards making his way under the blankets, pushing me aside so he could snuggle between Meagan and me. As he made himself comfortable, I watched Meagan sleeping so peacefully. She had truly been a ray of sunshine in my dark life. I was indebted to her for the joy she continued to bring to me. Ziggy's warm, furry body radiated heat upon us. He snuggled against my chest, pushing his paws into Meagan's back. As I closed my eyes, the biggest grin formed upon my face. I quickly fell into a deep, restful sleep. I didn't have to hope for a night of beautiful dreams, because I was already living mine. Life was perfect.

There are moments of such pure, sublime, unparalleled perfection that they will force you to close your eyes and hold on to them as best you can. Life is a series of these moments. Everything else is just waiting for them.
- Iain Thomas

Chapter Seventeen: Bon Appétit...

Being deeply loved by someone gives you strength,
while loving someone deeply gives you courage.
- Lao Tsu

It was really quite remarkable. In just the few short months since our little family was formed, we had grown together amazingly well. Recovery was in full swing for both Ziggy and I. With Meagan's help, and loving support, we both trudged forward in our battles for acceptance, happiness, and unconditional love. They were battles, that for the moment, we were winning.

Ziggy's once malnourished frame was now full and muscular. He had turned into a beautiful dog. He had the muscular frame of the Pit-Bull, while mixing in the gorgeous features of the Basenji. His body had recovered at a remarkable rate. His rib cage was no longer visible. His spine was covered, and even his hip bones had a decent amount of meat residing on them. He was a far cry from the skinny dog we had rescued. Maybe it was all the Fritos we fed him, I can't be sure, but whatever it was, it was working.

As he was recovering physically, I was recovering mentally. We seemed to be working in unison. I always believed we were connected on a much deeper level than I could ever truly understand. As I went, he went. As he went, I went. That connection could be seen and felt, but it was impossible to describe. Our souls were intertwined, dependent on one another for survival and healing.

As I admired my dog's new look, I couldn't help but think of the numerous times when he helped himself to some of my snacks that he shouldn't have. Each one of those snacks surely helped to fatten him up to where he was today.

The first time I seriously rolled my ankle while playing basketball, I was lucky enough to be the recipient of a week on crutches. The first two days, the pain was pretty severe. In reality, I was probably just a big wimp, but I thought it was pretty severe. I decided on the first day that I was going to spend the entire day on the couch. I was going to get up as little as possible, and Ziggy would obviously keep me company.

Before Meagan left to go out to lunch with her mom, she brought me a half gallon of ice cream. I knew I would be sick, but

I didn't care. I was going to eat as much of that half gallon as possible. As I dug into the mint chocolate chip ice cream, Ziggy kept getting closer to me, sliding his underweight frame towards me. As I ate the ice cream, I would occasionally let him lick the spoon. It was a ritual that he accepted very quickly. When we had finished off about half the ice cream, I felt sick to my stomach. My ankle was killing me. My stomach was too. I had just participated in polishing off more ice cream in one sitting than I usually ate in a month.

As I hobbled on my crutches to the restroom, I didn't think anything of leaving the ice cream carton on the coffee table. When I returned, Ziggy's head was buried deep inside. He was helping himself to the delicious mint chocolate chip ice cream. He had knocked the entire carton off the table, and he was pushing it around the room as he licked. Ice cream coated the top of his head and his floppy ears.

Laughing hysterically, I watched as his head got stuck in the carton. He attempted to quickly take a forceful step backwards to remove his head. He lifted his head, and the carton came completely off the ground. His snout and face were still trapped inside. He swung his head from side to side, trying desperately to get out, but the carton would not budge. After struggling for a few minutes, he gave up and lowered his head until the carton was back on the ground. He was defeated. He was embarrassed. He was covered in ice cream.

He started to whine, slowly at first. He cried for me to remove his face from the carton. For a moment, I just laughed. After all, he had put himself in this predicament. His whining continued, growing louder. Still, I couldn't move. The laughter was reminding me of all the ice cream I had eaten. After a couple minutes, he stopped whining and decided to continue eating the ice cream. I figured it was probably best to remove him from the sweet, sugary goodness. As I did, a proud face covered completely in ice cream was revealed.

That night, we were both as sick as dogs...literally. He was as sick as a dog, and I was as sick as him. The half gallon of ice cream had almost been completely polished off. We laid together, and we groaned as our tummies tried not to explode. I felt too sick to even get up to put the rest of the carton away, but every time I looked at it, I laughed.

That was the first time that Ziggy helped himself to something he shouldn't have, but it surely wouldn't be the last. Although he knew it was wrong, like the birds, he just couldn't resist.

On another occasion, a day after Meagan had gotten her wisdom teeth extracted; she decided to make a plate of scrambled eggs. For anyone who has had their wisdom teeth extracted, it is usually not a very fun experience. When you finally feel up to doing some things for yourself, it is a pretty monumental task. When Meagan made herself some eggs, she was pretty proud of herself. Ziggy was proud of her too, but he wanted to show her just how proud.

On her way to her bedroom to get her painkillers, she left her eggs on a TV tray in the living room. When she came back in the room, Ziggy was playing cliff hanger. He was helping himself to a mighty fine plate of eggs. He had one paw on the TV tray, another on the couch, and another on the chair. As he attempted to continue his miraculous, acrobatic, balancing act, he used his last available paw to push scrumptious scrambled eggs towards his drooling mouth. As he shoveled eggs into his mouth, he got spooked when Meagan entered the room. In his panic, the eggs, the TV tray, and his body went spiraling down to the floor in a massive crash. He stayed there, like a turtle caught on his back. As Meagan approached, he flailed his legs in a desperate effort to turn over. When he couldn't, he just stared up at her. He gave her that innocent puppy dog look that he had perfected over the past couple months. As she looked at him, irritated and disappointed, he belched.

Meagan, attempting not to smile, couldn't help but laugh. It sent an intense pain radiating throughout her mouth. The tears formed in her eyes. Whether they were tears of pain or laughter, I couldn't tell. They were probably a combination of both. As I watched this hilarious exchange, I couldn't stop smiling. Ziggy, whether behaving or being a serious pain in the ass, was truly a joy to watch.

Ziggy loved his steady diet of Fritos, mint chocolate chip ice cream, and scrambled eggs. Dog food was not a priority. It wasn't a highly desired dish for him. He was the pickiest dog when it came to dog food. When we first brought him home, he would turn up his nose at the dog food we purchased for him. We tried Science Diet, Pedigree, Ol'Roy and most others. We tested samples and listened to suggestions, but the malnourished dog wasn't interested. After all, scrambled eggs were a much tastier breakfast.

Ziggy's extreme pickiness was frustrating. After hundreds of bags of food, we decided to try Kibbles & Bits. I even demonstrated to him how to eat them. When he finally gave in, we were in for quite the surprise.

When we went to work for the day, Ziggy would normally just lounge around the house. He would lie in the big front window, basking in the sun, eagerly awaiting our return. When we would finally return, he would push his snout against the glass, fogging up the window. He would start prancing back and forth from one side of the couch to the other. His tail would swing fiercely with great excitement. Often, he would slip and his body would be sent crashing down to the couch. The goofy dog would waddle like a turtle until he finally centered himself enough to stand back up.

As we came inside, rather than greet us on the couch as he usually did, he urged us to follow him. He proudly strutted in front of us. When we entered the bedroom, the display of his work was truly remarkable. Our entire room, from one edge to the other, was covered in Kibbles. The Bits were gone, but the Kibbles were absolutely everywhere.

Ziggy was a casual eater. In an effort to help him gain weight, he had a large dispenser that allowed him to eat as he pleased. There were positives and negatives to this, but it was what the vet suggested.

It was definitely a negative this time. Ziggy decided to pick out all of the orange stick and twisty green Bits. He used his paw to push all the food out of his bowl so more would fall from his dispenser. Like a Special Forces operative, he would seek out only the Bits he desired. The remainder of the dog food was strewn across the room. The useless food stained the carpet red.

Over the next few days, we found Kibbles everywhere. There were Kibbles in the closet, in our bed, under our bed, in the entertainment center, in his bed, and under the desk. There was not, however, a single orange or green Bit to be seen. He had made sure to find every single one of his favorite Bits.

Ziggy, even when he was misbehaving, which was often, had a charm about him. He would gaze up at you with those big, dark eyes. A sense of pride always resided on his face. Whether he was stealing ice cream and scrambled eggs, or playing search and rescue with his Kibbles & Bits, he made sure he did it to the fullest. That was life for him. It made no sense for him to go halfway, and through his example, I started living the same way. That's correct; I stole ice cream and scrambled eggs. I picked all the marshmallows out of the Lucky Charms, but I learned how to do it from Ziggy, and that made me smile with joy.

His courage to face life inspired me. His friendship made me feel whole. His love made me strong. Loving him gave me hope. Loving him gave me the courage to face the future. As I loved him unconditionally, I wasn't afraid to start pouring love out to whomever I came in contact with. I wasn't afraid of pain and regret. Love began to ooze from my soul, and while I didn't understand it, I liked it. I liked it a lot.

You have within you more love
than you could ever understand.
- Rumi

Chapter Eighteen: Simple Pleasures...

Love is the discovery of ourselves in others,
and the delight in recognition.
- Alexander Smith

Ziggy and I were two peas in a pod. My love for him went way beyond the simple fact that he was my dog. It went beyond the fact that he was saving my life. My love for Ziggy grew, to an immeasurable level, when I saw myself in him. From that very first day that we locked eyes, I felt like if I were a dog, I would have been Ziggy. Similarly, if Ziggy had been a human being, he would have been me. He would have been a much better version, but still, he would have been me. That simple but complicated fact completely changed our relationship.

I was delighted by his recovery, because that meant I was recovering. I was delighted by his love, because that meant I was loved. I was delighted by his happiness, because that meant I was happy.

Ziggy's placement in my life was perfectly timed. While it wasn't flawlessly executed, our bumpy road to solace and understanding was slowly being paved with simple moments of happiness.

Throughout my life, I have felt like certain people were sculpted specifically for me. Without a doubt, a higher power, specifically and painstakingly, took the time to construct my father for me. For some reason, he just understands me better than any other human on this planet. He always has, and it is a safe bet that he probably always will.

God took a little more time on Meagan too. Using his amazing hands, He created her with me in mind. He knew that I would need an extremely special person in order to protect me, to love me despite my flaws, and to help guide me on this journey. Without her, I would be lost. Without her, death would have been welcomed. With her, I pushed forward.

Then there was Topher. He was one of those rare people that you meet and just click with. He was placed in my path when I needed him most. The blueprint was laid out, studied, and executed. He was there for me despite his own circumstances. He looked past our predicaments in order to help me understand myself.

Lastly, there was Ziggy. There was really no way to explain it. Words cannot describe it. True justice wouldn't be served. I will always be of the belief that Ziggy's previous life of pain and struggle was purposely given to him, so he could help me. If I hadn't seen myself, battered and broken, in Ziggy, then I would have never adopted him. The recognition of myself in him, and the recognition of himself in me changed our lives. It brought us together when we were both in the lowliest of circumstances.

People are not the only things placed in our lives when we need them most. Sometimes, it is a pet that takes the role of our perfect guardian angel and best friend. While my pops, Meagan, and Topher all molded me, and helped shape my recovery, Ziggy held the torch. He led the way, igniting a furnace of love within my heart. He refined me, melting down my sharp, jagged edges, smoothing my heart, and injecting color into the blandness that I had allowed to become my life. He did this in so many ways, not all of which I can put into words.

His zest for life oozed from him. It was a refreshing take on the troubled world that, at one point, I viewed as tasteless and unforgiving. The simple act of playing fetch with his squeaky soccer ball would bring unrivaled happiness that would obliterate any chances of darkness.

He loved that little soccer ball. It was his prized possession. I can vividly remember the day that he selected that damn squeaky ball. It was a warm day. Ziggy panted in the car as we made our way into town. He would, on occasion, sneak his snout up from the backseat until Meagan passed him a Frito. He loved riding in the car, and most of the time, he refused to sit in the back. He would whine at, and nuzzle Meagan, until she granted him access to the front seat. When she did, he would fly into action, making her lap his new spot.

This behavior was a catch-22 for Meagan. She loved Ziggy very much, but when he sat on her lap, he refused to sit still. By the time we arrived, she would be covered with his fur. Still, for his enjoyment, she usually allowed him to sit with her. As we pulled into the Petsmart parking lot, Ziggy eagerly pushed his snout against the window. He whined at the dogs he saw. He loved the other dogs, and he always wanted to play with them.

When we entered the store with our little friend, I could feel eyes upon us. At this point in time, Ziggy was still extremely malnourished. People gave us dirty looks, and looked upon him with pity. Sometimes, I would shout throughout the store...

"He's a RESCUE!" But, in the end, I didn't care what people thought.

In the store, Ziggy was unusually skittish. But, when we got the aisle of balls and toys, he lit up. As we talked with an older lady about him, he began digging through a basket of toys. He spread toys all over the aisle until he got to the soccer ball. There he stopped. He took the soccer ball in his mouth, proudly squeezed it a few times and sat down. He was satisfied. He had chosen his toy, and he was thrilled.

Most of the time, he would be the only one thrilled by that selection.

He would squeak that damn ball for hours on end. He would squeak it until it drove me absolutely mad. At night as I laid in bed, I would hear the constant squeaks coming from his bed. The high pitched noise would penetrate the silence of the night, and I would almost pee my pants on a nightly basis. Even when I knew it was coming, it would scare the hell out of me. He would wait until the lights went out for the night, and as soon as they did, he would squeak the ball over and over again.

Every single night, I would have to take away his squeaky ball, and I'd place it somewhere he couldn't reach. He would sit and cry at the dresser, or the night stand, or whatever location I had selected. After a couple pathetic whines didn't work, he would try to coax me into getting it for him. He would try to bribe me by snuggling close to me, kissing my face, and whining quietly. He was persistent, but he would eventually give up and just fall asleep.

In the morning though, he would be back to the dresser, or the night stand, and start the whining process all over again until his precious soccer ball was returned to him. He grew an attachment to that ball. I think it helped him cope with everything that had happened. It was something that was his, and his, alone. He never lost that ball, always making sure to have it with him whenever he could. If he couldn't bring it with him, he would place it neatly in his bed so it would be available upon his return.

Such was life for Ziggy. When he connected with something, he held it tight. He yearned to keep it close, so at times, when his soccer ball was out of reach, I became his soccer ball. It was the least that I could do. After all, he was mine.

One thing that Ziggy loved as much as his soccer ball, and his flocks of birds, was fluff. He loved to tear stuffed animals, limb from limb, in order to pull all the stuffing out of their insides. He loved to get the fluff out of his toys. We would raid the dollar store shelves of their bunnies and bears, so Ziggy could create his great masterpieces of carnage. Legs of bears and heads of bunnies would be sprawled across the floor. Their insides would hang out of his mouth, and be tracked across the house. He loved every single minute of it.

On Christmas, we acquired the massive cardboard box of a new refrigerator from a neighbor. With the box in hand, Meagan and I filled it completely full of fluff. We used bags and bags of fluff. We destroyed old stuffed animals from yard sales and our old couch pillows. We filled the box halfway with fluff. We placed a stuffed, quacking duck in the middle, and then continued filling the large box to the brim. As we laid the box on its side, the duck would start quacking incessantly. It would drive Ziggy absolutely crazy. He would sniff wildly from one side of the box to the other. He would start digging rowdily at the carpet trying to find any way possible to get inside the box. He clawed at it and whined. When we finally opened it for him, it truly was Christmas.

Ziggy dove in, grabbing massive amounts of fluff with his snout. He pulled the clumps of fluff apart, retrieving it from the box as fast as he could. The duck continued its obnoxious quack, which only drove his desire to remove the fluff faster. Fluff was flung from one side of the room to the other. Still, he continued to push his way forward, climbing, and clawing through the box like a dog possessed.

When he finally reached the quacking duck, I have never seen a head get torn off a body so quickly. As it did, the quacking was instantly silenced, and more fluff filled the room. We spent the entire morning, surrounded by fluff and full of smiles, as we watched Ziggy bound through it for hours. When he was finally worn out from creating his masterpiece, he took a mouthful of fluff in his snout, carried it into his new box and curled up for a much needed nap.

While the morning's activities may have seemed like no big deal, it was instances like those that made me contemplate how we had gotten here. As much as I regretted parts of my life, I was realizing that each building block, even the difficult ones, helped land me here. Without those struggles, I wouldn't be me. Without those hardships, I wasn't sure if Ziggy and I would have ever connected. Those thoughts always made the process of working to forgive myself a little bit easier. While I still hadn't completed that process, Ziggy was urging me to continue the process of working on it. The one major regret I had, the initial attempt to take my own life, was quickly becoming the one thing that was allowing me to change my life. That regret was allowing me to heal.

Maybe all one can do is hope to end up with the right regrets.
- Arthur Miller

Chapter Nineteen: Spring Time Sadness...

It has been said, 'time heals all wounds.' I do not agree. The wounds remain. In time, the mind, protecting its sanity, covers them with scar tissue and the pain lessens. But it is never gone.
- Rose Kennedy

Every year, as the cold grip of winter loosened, a strange sadness would always prevail within me. I guess a lot of people feel sadness as the holidays wind down, but for me, it was different. The depression, for the first time in months, started sprouting its powerful buds again. The spring sunshine helped encourage it along as the mourning set in.

January was always the hardest month for me to get through. The week of January 13th was devastatingly hard. As I sat in my room, reviewing my journal, tears filled my eyes as I thought of Jamal. His was a young, beautiful life that was never given a chance. He was taken from this world far too soon. So, in January, I was selfish. I was distraught. I would struggle.

My first attempt at taking my own life was in the dark, cold month of January, and although it was a year later, there were suddenly those deep dark inklings again. Despite all the goodness in my life, the pain bombarded my senses, and took hostage of my thoughts. I hadn't felt like this for so long. I tried to snap out of it, but it wasn't working. Despite Ziggy's best efforts, I was in a chasm that I couldn't seem to climb out of.

Around the same time that my sadness was in full bloom, Ziggy had developed some horrific allergies. His body's reaction to them caused him a number of issues. He rubbed his poor eye until the surrounding fur was completely removed. He rubbed the skin around his eye raw. It turned disturbingly red. It swelled and looked horribly painful. Once again, it was as if Ziggy's outward appearance was matching my inner feelings. He always seemed to suffer physically when I suffered mentally. I felt tragically guilty because of that.

I began to refuse to take my medication. I felt it was to blame for my horrific thoughts. Without the medicine, I felt that I would be able to function better, and hopefully leave the suicidal ideations behind. At least that was my hope. That night, as I sat with the bottle of pills in the bathroom, I couldn't decide whether I should just take them all, or if I should pour them down the toilet. As I contemplated my predicament, a paw flashed under the door. A whine could be heard from the other side. The whining grew more intense by the second. He stretched his paws as far as he could. He scratched dramatically at the door until I finally turned the cold metal handle to let him in. When I did, he just sat next to me. He didn't attack me with kisses or jump in my lap. Instead, he calmly gazed up at me with a concerned look on his face. He tilted his head from side to side, wondering why I cried.

Once again, in my moment of need, my furry little friend made my irrational thoughts go away. Shaking, I unscrewed the lid, and poured the pills in the toilet. With a splash, they sank to the bottom of toilet where they rested.

I smiled at Ziggy as I stared down at them. Putting his paws up on the rim of the toilet, he peered into the large ceramic bowl with me to see what I had just done. He looked pleased. The tears, the ones that consumed my eyes all too often were returning. I moved the silver lever on the toilet and watched the pills cyclone around the bowl as they were flushed away. I closed the lid, and just sat there with Ziggy's head resting on my knee. I patted the top of his precious head, and I wondered what would have happened if he hadn't been there.

The number of times he intervened, the number of times he helped change my thoughts, the number of times he just showed me that silent, unconditional love that I needed were too many to count.

As spring moved along, Ziggy's allergies got worse. While I had stopped my medications, Ziggy started his own regimen of pills. The vet prescribed him the extremely high powered steroid, Prednisone. At first, the Prednisone made his life bearable. The swelling in his eye receded drastically, and in time, the fur grew back. Like any medication though, the list of side effects was extensive and complicated. In the end, the side effects were absolutely horrible. Ziggy began to balloon up as he carried so much weight. He lost energy; he lost that pep in his step. He began to struggle.

While Ziggy started his downward spiral, I was rocketing upwards. After January's incident, I was alright. I was back on the path to recovery. I had stumbled backwards, but I continued to look forward. Ziggy, however, started looking back.

It was weird, almost ironic, and difficult to comprehend. For the first time in our unique relationship, there appeared to be a slight disconnect between us. After the first couple weeks of our companionship, we had always been on the same page. Connected. Together.

Charting our recoveries, we had always made our strides together. When we hit peaks, we stood upon them together. When we dipped, we dipped together. The valleys in his recovery were also my valleys. We stepped backwards together. We pushed forward together. It was always done in unison.

As I began to push forward, rocketing towards recovery, he began to slowly distance himself. I could feel something was wrong, but I could not understand it. I felt guilty. I felt incomplete. Maybe, I needed to step back, and stay on course with him. He had always stayed the course with me. I didn't know what to do. I was confused, upset, and resentful.

I wasn't sure what I resented. I didn't resent Ziggy. I resented the step back that was being taken. I resented the fact that I didn't know how to handle it. I resented the simple realization that I didn't know how to recover without him taking the same steps I did. I tried to wait. I tried to stay back with him, but I couldn't.

As summer approached, Ziggy had already gained fifteen pounds due to the medications. He started to struggle to get around. The weight made it difficult for him to do the things we enjoyed. When we attempted to take him off the Prednisone, he would scratch his eyes until they started to bleed. With an impending lose/lose situation on our hands, we decided that Ziggy functioned better on the steroid although it came at a very high cost.

The Prednisone lowered his already fragile immune system, made him gain a considerable amount of weight, and he seemed a little sadder. He would often lie alone, on the bathroom floor, sleeping on the cold tile. As he began to distance himself, I could sense that something was very wrong. For him, that spring time sadness had followed him into the summer.

He would play on occasion, but he was not the same. Still, any time we attempted to stop the medication, he would rub his eye completely raw until it began to bleed. The vet worried about infections that could cost him his sight, so we continued using the medicine.

At night, when he was sleeping, I would sneak over to his bed, and lightly pet him. He would usually wake up just to kiss my cheek softly before quickly falling back asleep. I would watch him thoughtfully, and I wondered what he was going through. That unconditional love was still there, but he was struggling, and I was scared.

One night as I carried him to his bed, I cried. This couldn't be happening. This poor puppy had already suffered and survived so much. He had taken so much of my pain. He had consumed so much of my sorrow. All I wanted to do was take away all his pain, all his sorrow. I wanted to make him whole, like he had been making me. The desire was there, but I didn't know how to fix it.

The pain of January never truly went away. It followed me all the time, but it was usually contained in the back of my mind. For me, even with Ziggy, the pain of January would never fully disappear.

Healing doesn't mean the damage never existed. It means the damage no longer controls our lives.
- Unknown

Chapter Twenty: The Last Walk...

Dogs are not our whole life, but they make our lives whole.
- Roger Carcas

As Ziggy's struggles continued, my worries grew. A part of me sensed that our time together was wrapping up. I hated that feeling, but it was there. Part of me thought that maybe I was just being a pessimist, while another part of me, thought I was only being a realist.

My once energetic buddy was becoming a shell of his former self. Like me, when we started this story, Ziggy was now the one that was in serious trouble. The dog still loved me unconditionally, but you could tell he was in serious pain. He struggled to get around. While his waddle was quite cute, it was not good for him.

I still tried to keep him active in some small way every day. He could no longer send flocks of birds into a chaotic frenzy. He could no longer swim after ducks or steal ice cream. He could no longer jog, but he could, and did, walk with me. We would walk often and it helped us both. I was accepting his limitations, just as he had previously accepted mine. His were easy to accept, as my list of limitations had always been much longer than his.

One afternoon as we walked, Ziggy just stopped. He refused to go any further. He sat down on the sidewalk and whined. He held one paw slightly off the ground, refusing to put it down. Upon further examination, I found, and removed, a large thorn from the pad of his front paw. Still, even with it removed, he wouldn't move. He just laid there, looking up at me.

I tried to nudge him, but his refusals continued. He was spent, and despite my pleadings would not move any further. Like a whale stuck on the beach, he just laid there. Due to the tremendous amount of weight the medicine made him carry, a whale was not an exaggeration.

For a moment, I sat next to him on the sidewalk, allowing his head to rest on my lap. I softly caressed his head with one hand, while I held his paw in the other. I could feel my eyes beginning to produce tears. I held them back. For once, I was not ready to cry. I refused to release the fear and pain that was suddenly consuming me. I wouldn't accept it. Not yet.

For so long, he had carried me. If you looked back on our incredible time together, you would often only see four paws as he carried me. It was finally my time to repay the favor for him. While he had carried me figuratively, it was my time to carry him...literally. As I picked him up, I realized for the first time just how much the Prednisone had changed him. While I had watched him gain considerable amounts of weight, I don't think I ever fully realized how hard the change had been on him.

My once strong friend was getting weaker every day. Basenjis are known to suffer from Fanconi Syndrome which causes kidney failure. Between his genetics, and the continued use of the high powered steroid, I worried about him. His life had been such a struggle, and when the vet explained to me the possibilities of his health taking a turn for the worst, I didn't want to believe her. But, it was true. Time was catching up with him, and the truth was catching up to me.

As I carried his weak body, he licked my face calmly. His thank you was definitely welcomed. For the next half mile, we struggled as the weight of his body started to fatigue mine. I am sure that it was quite the sight. I was in flip flops and carrying a 70 pound Pit-Bull/Basenji mix down the side of the street. I laughed as people passed us. I was positive that they were laughing at me too, but I didn't care. I would carry him to the ends of the Earth if I had to.

The carrying of Ziggy was truly a symbolic act for me. As I carried him, I felt a rush of emotion overcome me. The resentment I had previously felt was immediately washed away. I didn't want to accept what was happening, but deep inside of me, I knew I had to. As I cradled him in my arms, I thought about all the other times I carried him. None of them were ever like this. Never would I have thought that the carrying of Ziggy could do so much for me. It was cleansing. It was cathartic. It was essential. It was emotional. It was a sanctifying release of realizations.

While the act was simple, it helped me feel like our journey was complete. He had carried me, and I had finally carried him. While I knew our walks were starting to come to an end, today's made me realize it more than ever before.

In Ziggy's life before me, he had struggled. He had prepared himself, suffering pain and hardship, in order to be able to help me. In Ziggy's life with me, he had been whatever I needed him to be. Now, Ziggy was once again giving me what I needed.

I worried more than ever before. His scared eyes locked on mine, and that look was worth a million words. None of which I wanted to speak.

An animal's eyes have the power
to speak a great language.
- Martin Bube

Chapter Twenty-One: Regrets...

Regret for the things we did can be tempered by time; it is regret for the things we did not do that is inconsolable.
- Sydney Smith

Ziggy's health continued to slowly deteriorate. His continued health struggles left me pondering what to do. I desperately yearned for him to get better, but I knew it wasn't going to happen. As I noticed the changes in his demeanor, I was saddened. He avoided our interactions, and he began to isolate himself. It was as if he was rejecting me all over again.

Meagan and I worried about our future with Ziggy. We discussed going back to the vet to make a decision regarding his future. Bad days, however, would be followed by good days. This left us hopeful that maybe he would come out of it. After all, he had been through and survived so much.

Meagan had planned a wonderful trip to Disneyland for us. I, however, cringed at the thought of leaving Ziggy behind. I feared for him and us. I was quickly becoming that irrational pet owner that refused to leave his side. I struggled watching him in pain, and I begged for the ability to take it all away. His fragile body needed my new found strength. I yearned for healing, but this time, it was for him.

As we left him behind with my parents, I couldn't get him off my mind. While I enjoyed Disneyland, I constantly wondered how Ziggy was doing. When I saw Pluto, I lost it. Ziggy had always been there for me, and I felt so guilty for leaving him. He was in great and loving hands. For me, that still wasn't enough.

When our trip was coming to a close, I was overcome by a deep sensation to hurry home. After some much needed convincing, Meagan agreed to leave early. As we prepared to leave, I received a call from my dad. Ziggy was acting strange, and my dad was very concerned. We immediately rushed home from Disneyland to be by his side. When we arrived at my parent's house, we found Ziggy, lying alone, on the bathroom floor.

His tail wagged slightly as he saw us. He didn't budge. His eyes were heavy, and he looked so incredibly weak. I kneeled down next to him, and I patted his head. I scooped his body up into my arms. I felt a deep sadness rush through my soul. Ziggy lifted his head and kissed my cheek, reassuring me of his love.

For the ride home, I gingerly laid him in Meagan's lap. She caressed his ears. He didn't move, but nuzzled his snout into her thigh. As I looked at her in the rearview mirror, I could see tears in her eyes. Still, I wouldn't accept the reality of the situation.

That night, we snuggled with Ziggy. We held him close and monitored him. As the night drug on, Ziggy appeared disorientated. In a panic, Meagan and I searched the internet and the Yellow Pages for 24-hour veterinarians. The prices were astronomical. We discussed selling my Playstation, pawning her promise ring, and taking out a payday loan to cover the costs. While we rushed around, Ziggy began to vomit. It was thick and yellow. After vomiting multiple times, he appeared to be doing better. He made his way to his bed and finally went to sleep.

Meagan and I laid in bed with tears in our eyes. We didn't know what to do. We stayed awake for as long as we could, watching our sweet puppy. In the morning, we would take him to the vet. In the morning, he would be alright. If we could make it through the darkness of the night, everything would work out.

Don't worry about a thing,
'cause every little thing gonna be all right.
- Bob Marley

PART III: A LIFE SAVED

"The bravest thing I ever did was
continuing my life when I wanted to die."

- Juliette Lewis

Chapter Twenty-Two: Ending With Love...

There is a sacredness in tears. They are not the mark of weakness, but of power. They speak more eloquently than ten thousand tongues. They are messengers of overwhelming grief...and unspeakable love.
- Washington Irving

I was awoken suddenly by the familiar sensation of a cold, wet nose pressed against my cheek. It was a comfortable feeling that I had become accustomed to over the past year. Every night I would be greeted by him in the same loving manner. The cold nose would always be paired with a warm kiss that would follow soon afterwards. But, for some reason, tonight was different.

He continued to nuzzle my cheek, pushing his snout firmly into me. I caressed his soft, floppy ear tenderly as I wiped the sleep from my tired eyes. He continued his dramatic urges, forcing me to sit up. I reached erratically towards the nightstand in a wild attempt to illuminate the room. As I did, he gingerly jumped off my bed and headed towards his.

As the light filled the darkened room, he glanced back at me with those big, dark, hopeful eyes, pausing for a second as he did, insisting that I follow. His actions were slow and disoriented.

I trailed along behind him and watched his methodical movements. As he struggled to climb up on his bed, tears filled my eyes. I lifted him softly, and placed him on his pillow. He spun in a cautious circle and wearily dropped to his bed. He moaned feebly as he looked up at me with those eyes, still full of hope and love. They beckoned me, gesturing me to come closer.

I sat on his bed. He used what little energy he could muster to climb into my lap. He nudged my neck as I squeezed him close. Tears streamed down my cheeks and fell towards him. I cradled his head in my hands as he struggled to lift it. I nuzzled my face against his, and he slowly licked the tears from my cheeks. It was something he had done countless times before, but this time was different. I couldn't help but wonder if this was the end.

Those thoughts were difficult to digest. They were thoughts that had run through my head on multiple occasions before, but this was the first time that they weren't about me. Ziggy's heart pounded wildly. It reminded me of the night I almost ended it all. The pounding refused to slow. I squeezed him. I hoped that somehow holding him in my arms would slow the dramatic beating. He wheezed, struggling to breathe. I lifted him in my arms as I began to shake with fear. As I brought him into my body, I buried my head into his neck. His wiry, golden fur caught my tears as they streamed from my eyes.

I felt his heartbeat begin to slow dramatically. The pounding, far less intense than before, subsided. He wheezed again. My heart pounded madly as it desperately tried to compensate for his. For the past year, he had worked tirelessly to compensate for the endless list of faults that followed me. He made up for every single thing that I lacked. Without him, I didn't know what I would do.

In a final drastic effort, he lifted his weak head and struggled to open his eyes. Disoriented, he urgently tried to kiss my cheek one last time, but he was far too weak. I placed my cheek against his cold nose, and he licked the tears from my cheek one final time. The scent of his breath was horrific, but I didn't mind. I breathed in his scent as he wheezed for breath. His eyes closed, and his body stiffened. The wheezing disappeared as his heart took its final beats. That heart that was so full of love and compassion stopped. I closed my eyes, letting the tears fall uncontrollably. My body shook as I tried desperately to find the beat of his heart, but it was gone. There, in my arms, he had taken his last breath. In my arms, his last heartbeat had been felt. In my arms, his limp, lifeless body resided. My tears found their way, like they always had, into the comforting home of his fur. His ears were soaked with my grief as they had been so many times before. This time was different, this was the last time. This time, I would have to handle the grief alone. Still, as I held his motionless body against me, it consoled me. Even in death, he comforted me.

I sobbed uncontrollably as his lifeless body laid motionless in my lap. I buried my head into him as the tears fell like rain from my eyes. I clutched a paw in one hand and squeezed it. I was desperate for any response, but I knew one would never come again. Through blurry eyes, I stared down at him. Through the shrieks of sadness, I whispered in his ear, "I love you Ziggy. Thank you for saving my life." With that, it was over. Life with Ziggy was done. The rest of my life was just beginning. He was more than just a dog; he was the dog who saved my life.

Even when a river of tears courses through this body, the flame
of love cannot be quenched.
- Izumi Shikibu

Chapter Twenty-Three: More Than Words ...

We cultivate love when we allow our most vulnerable and powerful selves to be deeply seen and known, and when we honor the spiritual connection that grows from that offering with trust, respect, kindness and affection.
- Brene Brown

Ziggy, the dog, the companion, the friend, the savior had changed my life. He changed it in so many ways that it would be impossible to relay and describe each and every one. It is an insurmountable task to put his incredible life with me into words. His impact on me was truly life changing. His life was an absolute miracle. His mission to save me was complete.

As I stared down at him on that final night, I couldn't help but be consumed by an intensely overwhelming sense of gratitude for that malnourished, goofy looking dog that accepted the mission that would ultimately define him. I was so thankful for that horrifically skinny, big eared, and wide eyed canine, the one that was full of fear. He had agreed to ride shotgun in the battle of my life. He navigated me to safety. He fought tirelessly with me against those feelings of inadequacy and pain. He loved me unconditionally. He loved me for me.

Even in those desperate final moments, as his life was coming to an end, he was more concerned about me than himself. His last ditch effort, using the final breaths he had been granted, was truly remarkable. Rather than spend those final inevitable moments alone, he made his way to me. He brought his pain to me. In that moment, he allowed me, in a small way, to repay him. As I held him, as he kissed me, as I stared into his eyes, there was an understanding. His mission was complete. Crying uncontrollably, as our eyes met, we understood the gravity of the situation. As he fought to stay alive, his eyes looked hopefully up at me. I had hugged him close and whispered in his ear, "I'm ok. Just let go Zig. It's time." With those words, he kissed my cheek one last time before letting go.

He had waited for me. Not until I was ready, did he leave. Even in his final moments, those where he should have been selfish, he made a final effort to make sure that I was alright. He checked on me, when I should have been checking on him. That was Ziggy. That was my best friend.

With his mission complete, he left me, knowing full well that he had helped me begin to heal. Through him, I was recovering. While my depression wasn't gone, he knew that I could make it on my own. He had provided me the framework of happiness. I simply had to patchwork the quilt, taking the time to fill it with memories, love, and gratitude.

I had been given a new start. As Ziggy's spirit of love penetrated my fragile soul, I was reborn. He had filled the holes in my heart with beautiful, timeless memories. The dog whose journey had paralleled my life wanted his final moment to be different. As he died, he yearned for me to live.

His death symbolized my rebirth. It was yet another priceless gift that he bestowed upon me. I felt his spirit within me. A piece of me had always been inside him, connecting us for it seemed to be our destiny. In his death, I became stronger than I could have ever imagined. While the sting of loss was painful, it didn't cripple me. In his death, I found life. I found the will to continue on without him by my side, but he would always live in my heart.

I sat on the porch, and I watched the sun rise. As the beautiful oranges and pinks danced in the sky, I gazed upwards as the beautiful spirit of my guardian angel ascended back to heaven. The beauty and the brightness of the morning could only be matched by the love and understanding of his miraculous spirit. As I sat there, a smile formed on my face. He had successfully brought beauty back into my life. He had restored me, erasing as much pain as he possibly could. While all my wounds weren't healed, many of them had started to scar over.

With Ziggy, I accepted my vulnerabilities. I had stopped running. I faced the pain and disappointment that once contaminated my life. I opened up to understanding, acceptance, and love. I opened up to forgiveness. I hadn't rescued Ziggy; he had rescued me.

I wasn't sure if I was going to be able to remember who I was, who I am, or who I could be without him. I was pretty sure that the next morning when I awoke, I would eagerly look to the corner of the room at his bed, only to be reminded that he was gone. I would have to relive his death all over again. I wasn't sure that I could handle that.

I was his person. He was my dog. We were like two trees, each uniquely different, but each cut from the same forest. What I lacked, he compensated for. What he lacked, I tried to make up for. Our friendship was special. It was as if it was forged in Heaven, long before either of our lives ever began.

My once tattered and broken heart had been pieced back together and bandaged tightly. It was healing. The process was slow, but it was underway. I was on the mend. As I walked down the sidewalk, I felt the astonishing warmth of his unwavering love. I smirked as I imagined his warm kiss on my cheek. I watched as my shadow continued alone down the shabby sidewalk. Despite everything that I had put myself through, I had survived.

Suddenly, my shadow was not alone. I watched two shadows come together as Meagan appeared beside me. She kissed me on the cheek. I turned to face her, and as I did, we kissed passionately. For a short second, I peeked with one eye at the two shadows in perfect harmony. Life couldn't get much better. If Ziggy had taught me anything, it was time to close my eyes. I just needed to start enjoying the ride. Sometimes, the shadows are the only things that remind us of the beauty of the light.

One day, in retrospect, the years of struggle
will strike you as the most beautiful.
- Chris Jones

;

My Story Isn't Over Yet.

Depression, Self-Harm, & Suicide Assistance...

Every 40 seconds someone in the world dies by suicide. Every 41 seconds someone is left to make sense of it.
- International Survivors of Suicide Day

Assistance for depression, self-harm, and suicide is available. If you are struggling, please reach out for help from a family member, friend, or one of the resources listed below.

Hotlines
National Suicide Prevention Lifeline: 1-800-273-8255

National Youth Crisis Hotline: 1-800-448-4663

Poison Control: 1-800-662-9886

Websites
Suicide Prevention Resource Center:
http://www.sprc.org/

American Foundation for Suicide Prevention:
http://www.afsp.org/

National Suicide Prevention Lifeline:
http://www.suicidepreventionlifeline.org/

If depression is creeping up and must be faced, learning something about the nature of the beast. You may escape without a mauling
- Dr. R. W. Shepherd

Connect With Me...

Amazon: Review Life With Ziggy on Amazon.

Facebook: www.facebook.com/lifewithziggybook

Share your thoughts, book reviews, and questions about the book on the Life With Ziggy: A Boy, A Dog & A Life Saved Facebook fan page.

Instagram: #lifewithziggybook

Share a picture of you with the book on Instagram!

Email: LifeWithZiggyBook@yahoo.com

Reach out to me via e-mail. If you have a desire to buy the book in bulk, contact me for special pricing.

If you enjoy our story, please share it with your family, friends, and co-workers!

Acknowledgments...

*Hope is not the conviction that something will turn out well
but the certainty that something makes sense,
regardless of how it turns out.*
- Vaclav Havel

This work was possible because of those special people that helped me make sense of my life. To each of you that stood by me in my darkest hours, thank you. During those times when I was ready to give up, a special group of family and friends stayed by my side. Regardless of my irrational and irritating behavior during the difficult times, each one stuck by me.

To my beautiful wife, Meagan, I don't have the words. You saved me. Without you, there wouldn't have been a Ziggy. Without you, there wouldn't have been anything left to save. Thank you for loving what was left of me. You taught me that love is real and everlasting. You are a special piece of my soul. Your unwavering support and unconditional love amazes me every single day.

To my boys, Boston and Braxton, one day you will read these words, and you will understand just how important love is. I love you both with every fiber of my being.

To my pops, Ed, you are my hero. I appreciate the shoulder you have always offered. I am thankful for the 2 a.m. phone conversations. You are the man and father that I hope to be.

To my mom, Syd, you are my inspiration; an example of endurance. You help me to look at the bright side of life. Your continual reminder that everything happens for a reason drives me crazy, but it couldn't be any truer.

To my brother and sister, Brandon and Ashlee, I am grateful for all nighters of Halo and late night Jack-in-the-Box runs. The laughter each of you bring to my life is one of the greatest gifts I've ever been given.

To my uncle and aunt, Darin and Jo, thank you for assisting with the proofreading. Thank you for the talk; I will forever cherish that night in my heart. Without that talk, this story may have been locked away forever.

To Paula and Lee, I appreciate you accepting me into your crazy clan. It is a wonderful group to be a part of. Thank you for allowing me to bring Ziggy into our lives.

To the rest of my family, each and every one of you played a role in getting me to where I am today. Without you, I would be lost. Because of you, I am whole. Because of you, I am alive. Because of each of you, I feel like life is worth living. That belief has changed my life.

To all of you reading and sharing my story, thank you for spending your precious time with me. Your support is overwhelming, heartwarming, and appreciated. It is always extremely difficult to share the deepest, darkest secrets that you have hidden in your closet, but a great group of supporters make it a little bit easier.

To Topher, "What happens in Vegas, makes you successful."

To Jamal, I don't have the words. Thank you.

To Ziggy, you saved my life. No words can describe my love for you. It is unconditional and eternal.

You write because you need to write, or because you hope
someone will listen or because writing will mend something
broken inside you or bring something back to life.
- Joanne Harris

About the Author...

There is nothing to writing. All you have to do
is sit down at a typewriter and bleed.
- Ernest Hemingway

Justin Barrow, Jammer to his closest friends, once tip-toed on the fringe of ending his own life while struggling with a severe case of depression. Reflecting back on his experiences, he realized that a book would not only be therapeutic, but that it would have the potential to help others overcome the disease and the stigmas that are attached to it. As a result, Justin debuts his first book, Life with Ziggy: A Boy, A Dog, & A Life Saved. A native Nevadan and graduate of the University of Nevada Las Vegas, Justin currently resides in rural Nevada where he trains staff to mentor troubled youth as a training officer. He is a loving husband, father of twins, proud uncle, dog lover, fan of the Boston Red Sox, sports enthusiast, and blogger (www.badideadad.blogspot.com). Justin's second book, A Game to Remember, is in progress. The story follows the Fenton family as they use baseball to fight the effects of terminal cancer and Alzheimer's on their family.

Writing is something you do alone. It's a profession
for introverts who want to tell you a story but
don't want to make eye contact while doing it.
- John Green

Made in the USA
San Bernardino, CA
10 January 2015